Dyslexia and Early Childhood

Taking a developmental approach, this accessible text addresses the ever increasing interest in identifying the characteristics of dyslexia in young children and reflects on the best way to reach and support these learners. Drawing upon current research, the author considers our current understanding of dyslexia and calls upon best practice to advise professionals, students and family members alike who seek to fulfil the potential of young children with, or showing the signs of, dyslexia.

This book considers key topics explored in current best practice and dyslexia research, including:

- the importance of the role of speaking, hearing and understanding language
- dyslexia in relation to other languages and orthographies
- dyslexia and overlapping characteristics, particularly dyspraxia
- the role of play
- identifying and assessing dyslexia in the early years.

Adopting a dyslexia-friendly position, Barbara Pavey acknowledges the ethics associated with a social model of disability, so that the focus is upon modifying teaching and learning, and respecting the views of children and parents throughout. This book includes assessment and practice strategies, good practice points, helpful ideas, first-hand narratives of dyslexia, pointers for further reading, resources and online tools, and will be of enormous practical use to anyone supporting a young child with potential or diagnosed dyslexia.

Barbara Pavey is an independent dyslexia consultant and an educational consultant.

nasen is a professional membership association that supports all those who work with or care for children and young people with special and additional educational needs. Members include teachers, teaching assistants, support workers, other educationalists, students and parents.

nasen supports its members through policy documents, journals, its magazine *Special*, publications, professional development courses, regional networks and newsletters. Its website contains more current information such as responses to government consultations. **nasen's** published documents are held in very high regard both in the UK and internationally.

Other titles published in association with the National Association for Special Educational Needs (nasen):

Language for Learning in the Secondary School: A practical guide for supporting students with speech, language and communication needs
Sue Hayden and Emma Jordan
2012/pb: 978-0-415-61975-2

Using Playful Practice to Communicate with Special Children
Margaret Corke
2012/pb: 978-0-415-68767-6

The Equality Act for Educational Professionals: A simple guide to disability and inclusion in schools
Geraldine Hills
2012/pb: 978-0-415-68768-3

More Trouble with Maths: A teacher's complete guide to identifying and diagnosing mathematical difficulties
Steve Chinn
2012/pb: 978-0-415-67013-5

Dyslexia and Inclusion: Classroom Approaches for Assessment, Teaching and Learning, 2ed
Gavin Reid
2012/pb: 978-0-415-60758-2

Promoting and Delivering School-to-School Support for Special Educational Needs: A practical guide for SENCOs
Rita Cheminais
2013/pb 978-0-415-63370-3

Time to Talk: Implementing outstanding practice in speech, language and communication
Jean Gross
2013/pb: 978-0-415-63334-5

Curricula for Teaching Children and Young People with Severe or Profound and Multiple Learning Difficulties: Practical strategies for educational professionals
Peter Imray and Viv Hinchcliffe
2013/pb: 978-0-415-83847-4

Successfully Managing ADHD: A handbook for SENCOs and teachers
Fintan O'Regan
2014/pb: 978-0-415-59770-8

Brilliant Ideas for Using ICT in the Inclusive Classroom, 2ed
Sally McKeown and Angela McGlashon
2015/pb: 978-1-138-80902-4

Boosting Learning in the Primary Classroom: Occupational therapy strategies that really work with pupils
Sheilagh Blyth
2015/pb: 978-1-13-882678-6

Beating Bureaucracy in Special Educational Needs, 3ed
Jean Gross
2015/pb: 978-1-138-89171-5

Transforming Reading Skills in the Secondary School: Simple strategies for improving literacy
Pat Guy
2015/pb: 978-1-138-89272-9

Supporting Children with Speech and Language Difficulties, 2ed
Cathy Allenby, Judith Fearon-Wilson, Sally Merrison and Elizabeth Morling
2015/pb: 978-1-138-85511-3

Supporting Children with Dyspraxia and Motor Co-ordination Difficulties, 2ed
Susan Coulter, Lesley Kynman, Elizabeth Morling, Rob Grayson and Jill Wing
2015/pb: 978-1-138-85507-6

Developing Memory Skills in the Primary Classroom: A complete programme for all
Gill Davies
2015/pb: 978-1-138-89262-0

Language for Learning in the Primary School: A practical guide for supporting pupils with language and communication difficulties across the curriculum, 2ed
Sue Hayden and Emma Jordan
2015/pb: 978-1-138-89862-2

Supporting Children with Autistic Spectrum Disorders, 2ed
Elizabeth Morling and Colleen O'Connell
2016/pb: 978-1-138-85514-4

Understanding and Supporting Pupils with Moderate Learning Difficulties in the Secondary School: A practical guide
Rachael Hayes and Pippa Whittaker
2016/pb: 978-1-138-01910-2

Assessing Children with Specific Learning Difficulties: A teacher's practical guide
Gavin Reid, Gad Elbeheri and John Everatt
2016/pb: 978-0-415-67027-2

Supporting Children with Down's Syndrome, 2ed
Lisa Bentley, Ruth Dance, Elizabeth Morling, Susan Miller and Susan Wong
2016/pb: 978-1-138-91485-8

Provision Mapping and the SEND Code of Practice: Making it work in primary, secondary and special schools, 2ed
Anne Massey
2016/pb: 978-1-138-90707-2

Supporting Children with Medical Conditions, 2ed
Susan Coulter, Lesley Kynman, Elizabeth Morling, Francesca Murray, Jill Wing and Rob Grayson
2016/pb: 978-1-138-91491-9

Achieving Outstanding Classroom Support in Your Secondary School: Tried and tested strategies for teachers and SENCOs
Jill Morgan, Cheryl Jones and Sioned Booth-Coates
2016/pb: 978-1-138-83373-9

Supporting Children with Sensory Impairment
Gill Blairmires, Cath Coupland, Tracey Galbraith, Elizabeth Morling, Jon Parker, Annette Parr, Fiona Simpson and Paul Thornton
2016/pb: 978-1-138-91919-8

The SENCO Survial Guide, 2ed
Sylvia Edwards
2016/pb: 978-1-138-93126-8

Dyslexia and Early Childhood
Barbara Pavey
2016/pb 978-0-415-73652-7

Supporting Children with Dyslexia, 2ed
Hilary Bohl and Sue Hoult
2016/pb 978-1-138-18561-6

Dyslexia and Early Childhood

An essential guide to theory and practice

Barbara Pavey

Routledge
Taylor & Francis Group

LONDON AND NEW YORK

nasen
Helping Everyone Achieve

First published 2016
by Routledge
2 Park Square, Milton Park, Abingdon, Oxon OX14 4RN

and by Routledge
711 Third Avenue, New York, NY 10017

Routledge is an imprint of the Taylor & Francis Group, an informa business

© 2016 B. Pavey

British Library Cataloguing in Publication Data
A catalogue record for this book is available from the British Library

Library of Congress Cataloging in Publication Data
Names: Pavey, Barbara.
Title: Dyslexia and early childhood : an essential guide to theory and
practice / Barbara Pavey.
Description: New York : Routledge, 2016.
Identifiers: LCCN 2015037885| ISBN 9780415736503 (hardback : alk.
paper) |
ISBN 9780415736527 (pbk. : alk. paper) | ISBN 9781315818443 (ebook)
Subjects: LCSH: Dyslexic children–Education (Early childhood) |
Teaching–Methodology.
Classification: LCC LC4708 .P377 2016 | DDC 371.9–dc23
LC record available at http://lccn.loc.gov/2015037885

ISBN: 978-0-415-73650-3 (hbk)
ISBN: 978-0-415-73652-7 (pbk)
ISBN: 978-1-315-81844-3 (ebk)

Typeset in Galliard
by Cenveo Publisher Services

This book is dedicated to

Gillian Mary Anderson

With thanks

Contents

Appendices 128

List of figures

Acknowledgements

I would like to thank Dianne Brown, Judith Pearson, Dr Margaret Meehan, Dr Mike James and Gillian Anderson, friends, colleagues and family for conversations and correspondence about dyslexia and Sophie Pugh for her work on play. I would like to thank Gill Trivasse for telling me about some of the practices she uses to help dyslexic learners, and I would like to thank Jan Shandera for allowing me to reproduce some of her embedded letters, for telling me about US resources and for reviewing chapters. Similarly, I would like to thank Mike Bromfield for allowing me to reproduce his mouth shapes drawings and Mike James for reviewing my understanding of coding so helpfully.

I am grateful to the people who have shared their narratives and conversations about their experience of dyslexia. These were anonymised, but all had their origins in real accounts; all best efforts were made to obtain permission for their use. The quotation from Greg Kearney on page 10 is from his article *I am profoundly dyslexic and one of the few adults you will find who admits to it,* published by Daisy Consortium Zurich, and available online at: http://www.daisy.org. It is included with the permission of Daisy Consortium. Where I have recommended resources, products or websites, I have chosen these because I have used them, or because people I know trust them, or I because I have researched them. There is no 'product placement' involved, but I always hope to provide readers with something that they can use the next day, and I hope that they will find these suggestions helpful.

I would like to thank NASEN for continuing to advocate for special educational needs and, finally, I would like to thank Alison Foyle, Senior Publisher at Routledge, Sarah Tuckwell, my liaising editor, and also Joy Tucker and Michelle Antrobus at Deer Park Productions for their continuing patience, encouragement and good advice.

About the author

Barbara Pavey was originally a primary school teacher before working in further education, secondary education and, finally, higher education. She became a special educational needs (SEN) specialist and SEN coordinator, then moved to an administrative role in two local authorities, contributing to, and then managing, the processes of statutory assessment. This was the means by which children with significant special educational needs were awarded additional resources; in that context, concerns about dyslexia featured strongly. On being awarded a research doctorate in Special Education in 2002, Barbara entered higher education as a lecturer at Swansea University. There she became responsible for training postgraduate dyslexia specialists, and went on to undertake similar postgraduate training in dyslexia for the University of Birmingham and for the Institute of Education, University College, London. Barbara continues to work and write in the field of dyslexia.

Introduction

Definition of the early years age range varies, but for the purpose of this book the age of the young children at its centre is taken as being anywhere from birth through to about seven years old. It is possible to think about developmental dyslexia in the context of the very young children within this range, even while literacy skills are still emerging, because so much more information has become available in recent years, some of it research-based, some of it describing personal experiences and testimonials. This means that where once parents, grandparents and caregivers were reliant upon scarce dyslexia expertise, now they might reasonably expect all practitioners to know about dyslexia, as they know about it themselves.

Increasingly, both practitioners and caregivers consider that the literacy education of a young child is a shared undertaking. We may not rush to an identification of dyslexia, but we can be vigilant for its early characteristics in young children. We can provide ourselves with the skills and techniques to help in ameliorating the effects of dyslexia, and we can encourage children to develop confidence, perseverance and resiliency in order to overcome it.

This book is intended to assist practitioners, parents and caregivers to find ways of helping children at this early stage. It provides information about how dyslexia is understood at the present time, how it is assessed and how early learning might be supported with sensitive observation and practice, if an adult becomes concerned that literacy is not developing as expected. The first six chapters discuss characteristics associated with dyslexia, and their possible overlap with wider aspects of learning, focusing upon the context of early childhood. The next four chapters cover emergent and developing literacy, mathematics and science, and play, together with creativity. These provide further information about developing supportive practices for children who experience potential or actual dyslexia in early years settings. Chapter 11 shows that dyslexia is a lived experience which must be respected, but which can also be aided. At the close of the book there is a fidelity tool based upon principles in the text. This is designed to help us to reflect upon our supportive practice, and to consider how we may enhance it.

Our understanding of dyslexia is still developing, but practitioners and family members can adopt dyslexia-aware practices from the start of a young child's journey into language and literacy, aiding the processes of strategy-building for children who may develop dyslexia. I hope that this book will interest readers and serve to help any who seek to reduce the effects of potential or actual dyslexia for a young child.

Barbara Pavey

Chapter 1

Understanding developmental dyslexia today

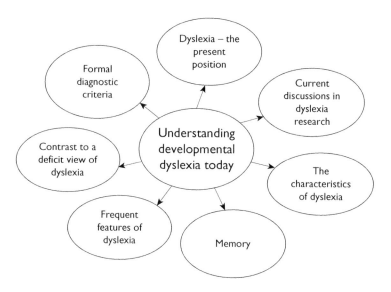

Good practice points

For good practice we need to:

1. update our dyslexia knowledge when the opportunity arises, knowing that dyslexia knowledge and understanding will continue to develop;
2. follow dyslexia-aware principles in all our practices;
3. watch for signs of difficulty or avoidance in early literacy tasks, and monitor these when they appear;
4. differentiate literacy tasks for children experiencing potential or actual dyslexia;
5. make note of, and respect, any concerns of parents, caregivers and practitioners about the possibility of dyslexia in a child.

Dyslexia: the present position

Dyslexia, as it is experienced by learners in educational settings, is known as developmental dyslexia, setting it apart from acquired dyslexia, which is the result of brain injury. It may also be described as specific learning difficulty (SpLD) While some aspects of dyslexia are now much clearer and can be regarded as firmly established, the questions surrounding dyslexia are by no means fully answered. Research continues to provide information from the reading, writing and spelling systems of all languages, while technological advances bring greater understanding of how our brains operate.

There has long been an understanding that dyslexia existed as a range; usually it has been described as mild, moderate or severe for a learner. There is strong support now for the view that dyslexia is part of a profile of reading that is continuously distributed across a population, although Ramus (2014) warns that evidence that there is no separate condition of dyslexia is by no means complete. The view of dyslexia as part of a regular range of reading has come about as a result of research which has established that there is neither a single dyslexia gene, nor any group of genes specific to dyslexia (see, for example, Lind *et al.*, 2010). Research continues to identify candidate genes; some studies identify 14 genes implicated in dyslexia (Carrion-Castillo *et al.*, 2013: 216), while others reviewing the field of study refer to 20 different genes and locations (Raskind *et al.*, 2013).

Some people learn to read (and spell) very easily, while others find it very difficult; most people fall somewhere in between. The question of whether dyslexia is a disability is one that gives rise to debate, but there is no question that for some people dyslexia is disabling, because of its severity. Dyslexia is not a concept that is easily defined, nor is it consistent in its presentation. This leads some authors to consider that it is not a useful concept, because it does not describe something that can viewed with certainty, beyond identifying it as a considerable difficulty with reading and spelling. This is the view of Elliott and Grigorenko (2014), although the authors do not dispute the idea that some people have extreme difficulty in gaining literacy skills. The authors point to the proliferation of terms and labels used to describe 'reading disability', but they also expect that dyslexia, as a name, will remain in popular usage for some time yet.

Current discussions in dyslexia research

Useful information about dyslexia comes from brain scanning studies, including the use of electroencephalogram (EEG), functional magnetic resonance imaging (FMRI) and positron emission tomography (PET) techniques. These have confirmed that developmental dyslexia is focused most clearly upon activation in the language centres of the brain, but that it is characterised by reduced activation at the learning stage, rather than by some unusual, other, dyslexia-specific characteristic. Brain imaging techniques also show that there may be activation of other areas of the brain. These indicate that, first, it is not exclusively the language centres that are involved in dyslexia and, second, a dyslexic learner's brain is working hard in other ways to overcome difficulties associated with literacy.

Much study has focused on phonological awareness and processing, and this has come to be respected as a core concept in dyslexia (Snowling, 2000). Phonological abilities are concerned with being able to perceive, recognise and apply the sounds of speech, as they are used in words and, particularly, as they are used in reading and writing. Among speakers of

English as a first language, this research focus has been longstanding and intense, and continues to be explored. However, current research looks at how theories interact (see, for example, Giraud and Ramus, 2013). To further complicate matters, issues can be interpreted through, and be influenced by, different underlying and competing views of teaching and learning.

A further difficulty in searching for a wider or more detailed understanding of dyslexia is that it cannot take account of environmental influences and differences in any but the broadest sense. The intense detail informing dyslexia research alerts us to the fact that dyslexia is not a simple matter, nor easily resolved. The range of discussion shows us that, at this stage, we should be cautious regarding simple explanations about the cause of dyslexia, and how to help it.

The characteristics of dyslexia

Much investigation has taken place as theorists, parents and carers, practitioners and dyslexic people themselves seek to make sense of the complexity of learning characteristics that go to make up developmental dyslexia. Increasingly, we are aware of the importance of learning environment, but we cannot really know much about any disruptions, absences, attitudes or educational shortcomings in a young learner's school progress. The only real common characteristic is that of reduced literacy, with a range of severity, and with a level of intractability that means it does not yield easily to regular teaching; it requires something further. Research has sought to identify subtypes, or clusters of characteristics that may be termed a syndrome, but Ziegler *et al.* (2008) confirm the view held by many practitioners, that categorising learners by subtypes is not especially useful. Dyslexic people have individual, personal literacy characteristics, so it is fair to say that, for practical and pedagogical purposes, all dyslexic learners are different.

There are, nevertheless, a number of characteristics commonly associated with dyslexia, which may be seen as children grow older and are faced continuously with literacy tasks. Not all children will demonstrate these characteristics; indeed, not all dyslexic children demonstrate a phonological difficulty. It is worth knowing about these differences, and how they may be addressed in order to help children to gain literacy skills. It is also important to dispel commonly held, over-simplified ideas when they are inaccurate. For example, being dyslexic does not necessarily mean a child cannot read; many dyslexic children learn to read, but they process literacy tasks more slowly than their peers and are likely to have greater difficulty in spelling. Similarly, dyslexia is not about reversing letters; some children will reverse their letters, but this is now seen as an aspect of the developmental delay that dyslexia represents – they are writing like younger children.

There are hopeful narratives about other characteristics experienced by dyslexic people, stating that perhaps they might be extraordinarily creative, or mechanically adept, or gifted in some way. This may well be the case, but it is not yet clear whether these assets are necessarily a direct result of dyslexia. Instead, they could demonstrate the wonderful qualities that can be exhibited by people when they are not constrained by literacy difficulty, and strive to advance in other areas. Dyslexic learners may also, themselves, be gifted and talented in ways that include literacy, but it is more difficult for dyslexic people to express themselves when literacy is their chosen outlet. Their efforts are not immediately obvious; they are, however, continuous.

It is not unusual for learners to experience other difficulties that occur at the same time, but sometimes these may be masked by dyslexia, or may not be considered when the focus is upon literacy. Dyslexia is a hidden disability; one of its characteristics that may go unnoticed is fatigue. Dyslexic learners have to work much harder to gain the same literacy skills as others and they may not ever gain the kind of automaticity or fluency which is expected when children learn to read, write and spell. This means that there is always an extra level of effort, and so there is an extra level of fatigue. Another complicating factor is termed the 'Matthew Effect' (Stanovich, 1986); the term refers to a parable in the Gospel of Matthew. Its relevance to literacy lies in recognising that skilled readers read more, and become more skilled, whereas struggling readers read less. As a result, a gap widens between these two groups.

Memory

Links between memory and dyslexia have been acknowledged for some time, with discussion generally focusing upon the role of working memory in gaining literacy skills. Working memory is described as the process that is involved when a learner has to work out how to do something from information he or she has been given. Baddeley (2003) divided working memory into further areas, particularly the phonological loop, which is concerned with speech and sound, and the visuo/spatial sketch pad, which is concerned with visual information. Both of these aspects bear a relationship to the process known as 'executive planning' or the 'central executive', which is concerned with planning, organising and carrying out of tasks. These are the thinking processes that we use to make things happen, related, in turn, to the things that we attend to unconsciously. It may be that interference with any of these processes could have a bearing upon what we understand to be the characteristics of dyslexia. Alloway (2011) finds strong links between working memory difficulties and specific learning difficulties, although she points out that while working memory problems might be a core characteristic, they are not a cause of dyslexia. Nevertheless, reduced verbal memory is described as one of the key features of dyslexia in the Rose Report (Rose, 2009).

The neuroscience of memory is not yet established; its characteristics are not yet clear-cut and well known. Recent research explores a view of memory as 'a common store with different activation states' (LaRocque et al., 2014: 1); this would allow for other aspects of memory. Two such aspects with importance for dyslexia are declarative and procedural memory. Michael Ullman defines declarative memory as that which 'underlies the storage and use of knowledge of facts and events' and procedural memory as that which 'supports the learning and execution of motor and cognitive skills, especially those involving sequences' (Ullman, 2004: 231). From this analysis, declarative learning is 'knowing that …' – it is knowledge that a learner can declare. Procedural knowledge is 'knowing how …' something is done – it is the knowledge for carrying out a procedure. Nicolson and Fawcett (2008) attribute dyslexia to difficulties in procedural learning, affecting automaticity, while declarative learning remains unaffected. A review of research (Lum et al., 2013) confirms the relevance of procedural learning for dyslexia, noting that it affects reaction time. However, the authors point out that a difficulty with procedural learning does not appear as a strong characteristic for every dyslexic person, and falls within a range.

Frequent features of dyslexia

Attempts to define dyslexia have literacy at their centre, but may also include discussion of mathematics, music and organisational and sequencing difficulties. Debate continues as to whether, when these are present, they are part of a dyslexic profile or a personal one. Furthermore, modern curricula are so strongly focused upon literacy skills, that dyslexia difficulties can spill over into other areas of teaching and learning, and undermine them. Bearing all these factors in mind, it is still possible to appreciate that, underpinning their difficulties with reading and spelling, dyslexic learners generally:

- have difficulty recognising and making connections between language sounds, spellings and writing patterns;
- find it hard to perceive any consistency in these;
- perform literacy tasks at the level of a younger child;
- do not experience literacy skills becoming automatic;
- may have good days and bad days for literacy activities;
- may forget what has already been learnt;
- may have difficulty with organising sequences;
- may experience co-occurring difficulties;
- may experience more fatigue than other learners;
- may frustrate and puzzle parents, teachers and themselves for these reasons;
- may have a considerable lack of confidence, even when it is not obvious.

There will always be a group of learners for whom literacy is especially difficult, and for some learners literacy will present insurmountable difficulties. With the move away from earlier discrepancy definitions, which compared one aspect of literacy with another, or compared levels of literacy with overall IQ scores, the remaining characteristics of dyslexia are descriptive ones. These include actual levels of reading and spelling, lack of response to regular teaching, slowness of processing and, particularly, the characteristic that it is very hard for a child to make literacy progress.

A contrast to a deficit view of dyslexia

Present-day approaches to disability have moved away from ideas about deficits, suffering and pity, towards recognition of the right of disadvantaged people to expect more effort to be made in order to provide them with full access. Social justice is expressed through recognition of the greater needs of disabled people, followed by positive action; treating everybody the same will not reduce a disadvantage. This principle is embodied in the social model of disability (Oliver, 1986), which holds that while individual people may experience impairments, it is society that disables through its practices and, even when these are improved, through its attitudes.

The practices of doing more for dyslexic learners are embodied in the dyslexia-friendly initiative. This was started by Neil MacKay and taken up in Wales, after which it became nationally and then internationally recognised. The British Dyslexia Association produced a free resource pack, *Achieving Dyslexia-Friendly Schools* (MacKay and Tresman, 2005) and developed a quality mark process to spread and implement dyslexia-friendly principles. Central to dyslexia-friendly practice is the understanding that what is good teaching for dyslexia is good teaching for all learners; practices that were previously seen as the work of dyslexia specialists have now found their way into mainstream education.

Understanding developmental dyslexia today is a continuously evolving task. In the world of dyslexia discourse there are competing psychological and sociological views, and there are perspectives that seek to reconcile these. Research continues to augment our understanding, and the identity of dyslexia as a specific learning difficulty changes with the revisions made in diagnostic criteria.

Nevertheless, there are some 'anchors', or constants within the discussion. One is that dyslexia describes literacy difficulty that falls within a range, so there is always going to be a small number of children who find literacy so difficult that it will be overwhelming and disabling. Awareness of the importance of phonological difficulty and reduced speed of processing also prove consistently to be core concepts in dyslexia. A further 'anchor' is provided by Morton and Frith's (1995) analysis of dyslexia theory; this provides a model of dyslexia which shows that, whatever the theoretical perspective, dyslexia consists of biological, cognitive and behavioural elements, all influenced by environment. Today, we consider that we may at least go some way towards identifying the characteristics associated with possible dyslexia at an earlier age; we do not expect to wait for reading and spelling failure. All these constants provide us with sufficient information to be vigilant for learners who are struggling. We can also make sure we listen to children themselves when they tell us about their literacy learning.

Formal diagnostic criteria

Discussions about dyslexia eventually turn to the diagnostic criteria for dyslexia or reading disability currently found in the *Diagnostic and Statistical Manual of Mental Disorders*, fifth edition (*DSM-5* or *DSM-V*), published by the American Psychiatric Association (2014), and the International Classification of Diseases, tenth revision, published by the World Health Organization (see, for example, WHO, 2010), with *ICD-11* due by 2018. These manuals are consulted by psychologists and paediatricians when making an identification or diagnosis. The International Classification of Diseases tends to be consulted in Europe, while the USA and UK tend to consult the *Diagnostic and Statistics Manual*. The classifications are not 'hidden' knowledge, but in general they do not tend to be part of the day-to-day work of educators. Ultimately, dyslexia definitions relate to the criteria embodied in the manuals, and these have changed or are changing, with the new editions.

DSM-5 does not include dyslexia as a particular disorder. Instead, it has a category of 'specific learning disorders', which includes reading and writing difficulties and mathematical difficulties. The literacy characteristics are defined as 'inaccurate or slow and effortful reading' and 'poor written expression that lacks clarity' (American Psychiatric Association, 2014). *DSM-5*'s literacy disorder does not cover spelling – similarly to the criterion in *ICD-11*, this is described as a specific learning disorder of impairment in written expression.

ICD-11 (Beta version) describes a developmental reading disorder, where the problem rules out other causes; developmental dyslexia is listed as a term by which this 'disorder' may be known. It is considered that a severe difficulty with spelling is a different disorder, part of a developmental disorder of written expression. Of particular interest is the fact that it notes the disorders as affecting the whole brain (WHO, 2012), moving away from the idea of a literacy difficulty being specifically located within one brain area.

While there are both similarities and differences in *ICD-11* and *DSM-5*, each diagnostic protocol now indicates that dyslexia is a term describing a reading disorder, rather than a separate condition in its own right, and *DSM-5* includes the view that 'specific symptoms, such as difficulty in reading, are just symptoms' (American Psychiatric Association, 2014). This is disappointing for commentators who identify unique qualities in dyslexia. It need not prevent us from respecting the learning difficulty that dyslexia represents, or the exceptional qualities that some people with dyslexia will develop. Both sources recognise that it is severity of the disorder that is disabling. Diagnostic criteria are reviewed on a regular basis and, in the meantime, research continues.

Dyslexia-aware principles: adopting a dyslexia-friendly approach

The dyslexia-friendly initiative expects that education authorities, schools and all members of staff should be aware of dyslexia, should know how to support children who experience it and should know how to advise parents and carers appropriately. However, even though much more is now known about dyslexia, there remains a strong attraction towards the idea of finding an intervention that solves a child's literacy problem, fixes it (preferably quickly) and brings a child back into the frame of regular teaching where there is no further concern, and no further need for intervention. The reality is that dyslexia is a lifelong characteristic that may be overcome, and for which strategies can be developed, but which cannot be eliminated. Practitioners can develop their own practice by adapting dyslexia-aware approaches and techniques for teaching literacy to children in the early years, such as:

* using a multisensory approach;
* giving instructions in a small number of steps;
* using over-learning: revisit, revise, repeat (with variation);
* using alternative ways of recording;
* using information and communication technology;
* using mnemonics, rhymes, songs, games;
* using drawing – both practitioners' and children's;
* using pastel-coloured backgrounds for print;
* using larger, plain fonts for print;
* looking for quality, rather than quantity;
* showing children where the learning is heading by telling them what the end point is, so that they can perceive the 'big picture';
* focusing on ability level not literacy level, and finding ways to let ability shine through.

Dyslexia-aware practice: good-quality written resources for young children

Making written resources and stimuli as clear as possible helps all young readers. However, dyslexic, or potentially dyslexic, children will be helped if clarity of this sort is maintained throughout their school lives. Practitioners can help their learners by making text as accessible as possible and for young readers this would include:

- checking the reading age of any material – for example, by using the readability tool in the Microsoft Word program (this is found via the spelling- and grammar-checking window, activated by clicking Options and ticking the readability box)
- using clear, clean fonts of a suitable size
- keeping text in small groupings, with clear spacing between them
- using visual material and keeping it close to the text
- giving short lists of key words, preferably separated – e.g. in a text box
- using tinted paper, unless there are learners in a group who experience visual impairment, and who will then need the strong contrast of black print on a white background.

In using the Microsoft Word readability statistics we should aim for:

- very few passive sentences, plus a Flesch Reading Ease score that is as high as we can arrange, reworking our text to meet these requirements;
- the lowest possible Flesch–Kincaid grade level. This is a US grade level and we add 5 to this to arrive at the approximate reading age for UK usage (Pavey, 2013a: 14).

Information and communication technology in early years settings

Information and communication technology (ICT) is an established part of modern life; there is a question as to whether children should be knowledgeable about ICT before they begin formal schooling. Writing from within the Australian context, Hesterman (2013) considered different approaches to early years settings, looking particularly at the way that ICT could be used to promote 'multiliteracies'. This concept describes an understanding of literacy which is wider than that which covers a traditional, language-based approach to reading, writing and spelling. The view is that children are growing up in a digital world and need to be able to navigate and create digital learning experiences.

Hesterman found that ICT resources were often available, but the way in which they were used depended upon the practitioners', or settings', particular educational point of view and also upon the way resources were provided and maintained. She also found that practitioners benefited from being able to discuss ideas and techniques with each other, but that this was not always possible.

Generally, Hesterman found that computers were used as a kind of play, where children could choose from among a number of activities. Sometimes they were used as an alternative form of conventional literacy learning, taking a traditional approach but using electronic means. There would be access, but often it was tightly controlled. In only one of her case studies was there a sense of 'multiliteracy', where young children were able to plan and carry out projects of their own using ICT, building projects that could be shared and appreciated within the class or group setting.

ICT access is important for learners who experience dyslexia as it allows them to replay and repeat items of learning in their own time and at their own pace. ICT presentation frequently makes allowances for dyslexia, providing for a change of colour in background or text and changes of font size to improve readability. A 'multiliteracy' approach, allowing even young children to create and share ICT projects, offered together with a dyslexia-aware perspective, would widen the scope for confident literacy learning for children who experience possible or actual dyslexia.

Learning games: Follow-the-Leader; Move Right; Left Side, Right Side – supporting left and right orientation

Dyslexic learners sometimes report that they remain confused between left and right; they may have to think about it rather than make an automatic response. These games can reinforce left and right discrimination.

a) *Follow-the-Leader*: children follow a command – 'right hand on right shoulder', 'left hand on right ear', etc.
b) *Move Right*: children sit in chairs arranged in rows. 'Change right' is called, and all the children move to the seat to the right of them, and the child at the end runs round to the now vacant seat on the left-hand end of the row. 'Change left' is called, and the opposite happens. The speed of the game can be increased, as fast as children can cope with it.
c) *Left Side, Right Side*: run to touch the wall nearest your left side – right side – point right – point left – swing right leg to right – to left – etc.

Adapted from McNicholas and McEntee (1991, 2004), no. 3: Left/Right Discrimination – Follow-the-Leader (p. 6) and no. 4: Left-to-Right – Moving Right (p. 6).

How can dyslexia be supported in these games?

*   For Move Right and Left Side, Right Side, learning can be helped if a practitioner doing the calling holds up a sign with a clear L or R (upper or lower case as preferred), fading this stimulus as the children become more familiar with left and right.
*   A practitioner can wait until everybody has arrived in the right place, before changing the instruction.
*   If someone makes the wrong move, they should not be called 'out', reprimanded, or made to feel embarrassed. Perhaps a practitioner might make the wrong move sometimes too, and a little shared laughter will keep the mood light.
*   If the same child makes the wrong move too often, they can be made the 'caller' until they are more secure with left and right.

Attitude, understanding, technique, empathy: professional knowledge

If a dyslexia-aware practitioner's professional knowledge combines 'attitude, understanding, technique, and empathy' (Pavey, 2013b: 2), characteristics of good practice would include:

*   *attitude*: being aware that while definitions and identifications of dyslexia may vary and change, in any group there are always likely to be learners with the potential for literacy difficulty, and it is our responsibility to help them;

- *understanding*: knowing that good teaching for dyslexic learners is good teaching for everyone;
- *technique*: being able to design teaching and learning experiences in a way that is helpful to learners who may experience dyslexia;
- *empathy*: being aware of language and literacy difficulty, fatigue, stress and apprehension, and appreciating that these may be present even at a very young age.

Recommended reading

1. MacKay, N. (2012) *Removing Dyslexia as a Barrier to Achievement* (3rd edn), Wakefield, SEN Marketing (www.senbooks.co.uk)
2. MacKay, N. and Tresman, S. (2005) *Achieving Dyslexia Friendly Schools Resource Pack* (5th edn), Bracknell, British Dyslexia Association, available online at: http://www.bdadyslexia.org.uk/ (training and accreditation section)
3. Matterson, E. (1991) *This Little Puffin*, London, Penguin

Useful websites

1. https://www.gov.uk
   Information from the English Department for Education (DfE) is held on this site. A useful, free child development resource here is the Department for Education (2013), *early years Outcomes*. In a simple and easy-to-read format this outlines expectations of usual developmental progress, with a focus on literacy in section 4.
2. http://thedyslexia-spldtrust.org.uk
   The Dyslexia-SpLD Trust is an umbrella organisation for major dyslexia organisations in the UK. Its website contains free resources for practitioners, parents and carers. Most importantly it contains the Professional Development Framework, a free web-based tool to help individuals and schools develop their practice in support of learners who experience dyslexia, or possible dyslexia (see micro-site on right-hand side of home page). Registration is required.
3. http://www.tts-group.co.uk
   There are a number of companies who produce resources for practitioners. TTS has a specific early years catalogue with resources linked to the English early years Framework, and designated early literacy materials.

MY DYSLEXIA EXPERIENCE: LEFT AND RIGHT

I can only tell left and right because I wear my watch on my left hand, and check constantly. Reading is an activity which requires you to track left and right across the page, but I get bored working out letter by letter and then lose track which direction am I going. There are many letters that are different only by direction: bs and ds, qs and ps, so sorting them out each time they are encountered becomes an incredibly time consuming process. (Greg Kearney, 2014)

References

Alloway, T. (2011) *Improving Working Memory*, London, SAGE

American Psychiatric Association (2014) *DSM 5 Development*, available online at: http://www.dsm5.org/

Baddeley, A. (2003) Working Memory and Language: An Overview, *Journal of Communication Disorders*, 36, 189–208

Carrion-Castillo, A., Franke, B. and Fisher, S. (2013) Molecular Genetics of Dyslexia: An Overview, *Dyslexia*, 19, 4, 214–40

Department for Education (2013) *Early Years Outcomes*, London, DfE, available online at: https://www.gov.uk/

Elliott, J. and Grigorenko, E. (2014) *The Dyslexia Debate*, Cambridge, Cambridge University Press

Giraud, A.-L. and Ramus, F. (2013) Neurogenetics and Auditory Processing in Developmental Dyslexia, *Current Opinion in Neurobiology*, 23, 37–42

Hesterman, S. (2013) Early Childhood Designs for Multiliteracies Learning, *Australian Journal of Language and Literacy*, 36, 3, 158–68

Kearney, G. (2014) I am Profoundly Dyslexic and One of the Few Adults you will Find Who Admits to It, Daisy Consortium, available online at: http://www.daisy.org/stories/greg-kearney, accessed 30 October 2014

LaRocque, J., Lewis-Peacock, J. and Postle, B. (2014) Multiple Neural States of Representation in Short-term Memory? It's a Matter of Attention, *Frontiers of Human Neuroscience*, 8, Article 5, 1–14

Lind, P. Luciano, M., Wright, M., Montgomery, G., Martin, N. and Bates, T. (2010) Dyslexia and DCDC2: Normal Variation in Reading and Spelling is Associated with DCDC2 Polymorphisms in an Australian Population Sample, *European Journal of Human Genetics*, 1–6 January, accessed 31 March 2010 at: http://www.qimr.edu.au/

Lum, J., Ullman, M. and Conti-Ramsden, G. (2013) Procedural Learning is Impaired in Dyslexia: Evidence from a Meta-analysis of Serial Reaction Time Studies, *Research in Developmental Disabilities*, 34, 10, 3460–76

MacKay, N. (2012) *Removing Dyslexia as a Barrier to Achievement* (3rd edn), Wakefield, SEN Marketing (www.senbooks.co.uk)

MacKay, N. and Tresman, S. (2005) *Achieving Dyslexia Friendly Schools Resource Pack* (5th edn), Bracknell, British Dyslexia Association, available online at: http://www.bdadyslexia.org.uk/ (Quality Mark and Accreditation section)

McNicholas, J. and McEntee, J. (1991, 2004) *Games to Improve Reading Levels*, NASEN/Routledge

Morton, J. and Frith, U. (1995) Causal Modelling: A Structural Approach to Developmental Psychopathology, in D. Cicchetti and D. Cohen (eds) *Manual of Developmental Psychopathology*, New York, Wiley

Nicolson, R. and Fawcett, A. (2008) *Dyslexia, Learning, and the Brain*, Massachusetts, Massachusetts Institute of Technology

Oliver, M. (1986) Social Policy and Disability: Some Theoretical Issues, *Disability and Society*, 1, 1, 5–17

Pavey, B. (2013a) Supporting Learning, in B. Pavey, M. Meehan and S. Davis, *The Dyslexia-friendly Teacher's Toolkit*, London, SAGE

Pavey, B. (2013b) Understanding Learners with Dyslexia, in B. Pavey, M. Meehan and S. Davis, *The Dyslexia-friendly Teacher's Toolkit*, London, SAGE

Ramus, F. (2014) Should There Really Be a 'Dyslexia Debate'? *Brain*, 137, 3371–4

Raskind, W., Peter, B., Richards, T., Eckert, M. and Berninger, V. (2013) The Genetics of Reading Disabilities: From Phenotypes to Candidate Genes, *Frontiers in Psychology*, 3, article 601, 1–20, available online at: http://www.ncbi.nlm.nih.gov/, accessed 31 May 2014

Rose, Sir J. (2009) *Identifying and Teaching Children and Young People with Dyslexia and Literacy Difficulties*, Nottingham, DCSF

Snowling, M. (2000) *Dyslexia* (2nd edn), Oxford, Blackwell

Stanovich, K. (1986) Matthew Effects in Reading: Some Consequences of Individual Differences in the Acquisition of Literacy, *Reading Research Quarterly*, XXI, 4, 360–407

Ullman, M. (2004) Contributions of Memory Circuits to Language: The Declarative/Procedural Model, *Cognition*, 92, 231–70

World Health Organization (WHO) (2010), *ICD-10 Version: 2010*, available online at: http://apps.who.int/

World Health Organization (WHO) (2012) *ICD-11 Beta Draft*, available online at: http://apps.who.int/

Ziegler, J., Castel, C., Pech-Georgel, C., George, F., Alario, F.-X. and Perry, C. (2008) Developmental Dyslexia and the Dual Route Model of Reading: Simulating Individual Differences and Subtypes, *Cognition*, 107, 1, 151–78

Chapter 2

Who are the young children experiencing dyslexia and dyslexia precursors?

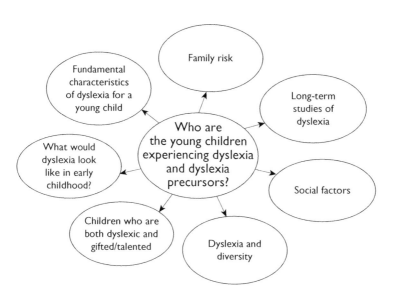

Good practice points

For good practice we need to:

1. recognise learners at risk of dyslexia and share any concerns with SENCO or specialist;
2. where children are at risk of dyslexia, pay increased attention to phonological knowledge, speed of processing (particularly the naming of items, objects and pictures) and letter knowledge;
3. link new learning to previous learning, as this provides context which supports understanding, helping new learning to be maintained;
4. provide opportunities for higher-order cognition, such as in planning, prediction, discussion of ideas and alternatives, and the making of aesthetic judgements;
5. put in a 'step' when learning falters.

Family risk

There has been considerable interest in identifying young children 'at risk' of dyslexia through the likelihood of their inheriting dyslexia traits. Before genetic research, family studies tended to be of two kinds: they either looked at family groups where a parent or other family members experienced dyslexia, or they looked at twins and adopted children. These early studies (see, for example, Scarborough, 1989) established that dyslexia was more likely to emerge as a result of genetic factors than as a result of environmental ones; dyslexia was shown often to be inherited. The level of heritability is now considered to be at about 50 per cent; Raskind *et al.* (2013) confirm that most studies place the likelihood of inheriting dyslexia at between 40 and 60 per cent.

Sometimes, dyslexia is present without any obvious connection to family members. This may be because mutation of genes has take place of its own accord, but it may also mean that family information about dyslexia is not known. We have only to look back for one or two generations to find that higher levels of school absence and earlier school-leaving ages, together with lack of the relevant knowledge, operated against identification of dyslexia. To this may be added the perceptions of older people that they were stupid, or judged to be so, because of literacy difficulties. Dyslexia was not part of the conversation.

Long-term studies of dyslexia

Our understanding of developmental dyslexia has benefited from long-term studies that provide evidence of the characteristics and processes involved in dyslexia. In a longitudinal study Shaywitz and her co-authors confirmed the persistence of dyslexia over time. While people who experience dyslexia can gain literacy skills, there is no real likelihood of their literacy becoming automatic in the same way as it does for people without dyslexia; it can be overcome but it cannot be made to disappear (Shaywitz *et al.*, 1999). More recently, two important studies have taken place, in Finland and Holland, focusing upon very young children who might develop dyslexia, following them through their school years.

Researchers involved in the Finnish Jyväskylä University longitudinal study of dyslexia (JLD) confirmed familial risk for dyslexia and concluded that very early predictors of pre-literacy skills could be found within a brain's electrical responses to tones and speech sounds at birth. The research team found that the best predictors of decoding (reading) accuracy and speed are phonological awareness, rapid automatic naming (RAN) and letter knowledge. 'Phonological awareness' refers to awareness of the sound structure of words, especially when they are spoken; rapid automatic naming refers to how quickly a person can name lists of items, retrieving the correct word from their memory; and letter knowledge is alphabetic knowledge – that is, the names and the shapes of alphabet letters. For spelling, the JLD found that the key factor is phonological awareness and, for understanding of text, the key factor is vocabulary. The team found that mothers providing supportive behaviour in play and prompting reading activities ('activating strategy') aid the development of literacy, as does the sharing of a book between a parent and a child. The team also found that being in a class might help, as well as the degree of interest in reading, but these findings were not quite so strong (Lyytinen *et al.*, 2008).

Like the JLD, the Dutch Dyslexia Programme (DDP) is a long-term study, building upon the JLD work by tracking three groups. These are made up of a group from families where there is at least one parent with dyslexia and where the children in the research develop dyslexia themselves; and a group from families where there is dyslexia but where the children did not, themselves, develop dyslexia. The third group is a control group, where there is no dyslexia in parents or their children (van der Leij *et al.*, 2013).

The study showed that at the age of one-and-a-half-years children with a dyslexic parent already differed from children without familial risk, both in the number of words they produced and the number of words in their vocabulary. As children were tested at later stages, the study found that the characteristics that made the difference in reading acquisition, and were therefore strong predictors of dyslexia, were phoneme awareness (part of phonological awareness, referring to the particular sounds from which words are constructed), RAN and letter knowledge, confirming the findings of other family risk studies. The authors of the DDP found that where children developed dyslexia, indications of these difficulties had been present before they had, formally, learnt to read.

In summarising their research, the DDP researchers concluded that dyslexia comes about as a result of a complex interaction of a number of factors plus environment. Of special note is the DDP finding that children who come from families with dyslexia, but who do not have dyslexia themselves, do better in literacy than dyslexic children, but not as well as children from families without dyslexia at all. The study concludes that a strong predictor of the severity of a child's dyslexia is the severity of their parent's dyslexia.

Social factors

Confirmation of the importance of the environment leads to a consideration of social factors; dyslexia has had a complicated relationship with these. It has been argued that dyslexia became prominent in education because of the demands of wealthier parents with knowledge of social and professional systems. They were seen as seeking explanations which did not rely on lack of intelligence if their children did not learn to read (Tomlinson, 2005). The prominence of dyslexia has been driven also by the ever-increasing importance of literacy in modern life. Nevertheless, rates of dyslexia and perceptions of levels of severity are considered to be higher in socially disadvantaged populations (Macdonald, 2009). This may reflect constraints created by lack of opportunity when a learner experiences literacy difficulties, but may also reflect the improved social capital that results from advantage. As Macdonald points out, 'Individuals with access to finance have more control over disabling barriers within contemporary society' (ibid.: 45).

Gender is also an issue. During the years when it was emerging as an identifiable learning characteristic, dyslexia was considered to be a characteristic of boys; several factors influenced this view. Whether it was because boys were more noticeable, or because they were noticed more, their literacy difficulties attracted greater attention, whereas now we consider that girls with dyslexia may be under-identified.

Advantaged social status can create a kind of 'polish' that looks like social coping, reflected perhaps in vocabulary choices. Girls as a group are also thought to have better coping skills, perhaps calling on friendships to support them in their classwork. In contrast, boys without these social coping strategies may be judged adversely if their difficulty is reflected in resistant behaviour. Practitioners will need to feel confident that assumptions and decisions about dyslexia are not made on the basis of social status or gender.

Dyslexia and diversity

Burns and Shadoian-Gersing define diversity as '[C]haracteristics that can affect the specific ways in which developmental potential and learning are realized, including cultural, linguistic, ethnic, religious, and socio-economic differences' (Burns and Shadoian-Gersing, 2010: 21). They point out that diversity is, increasingly, a significant part of developed societies, bringing changes that can enrich enormously our experience of modern life. Teachers need to be flexible, and may have to change their teaching and learning styles in order to cope with new demands. However, diversity training tends to be variable.

There is little discussion about ethnicity or diversity in studies about dyslexia; the view tends to be that dyslexia can affect anyone, regardless of social factors, but this is perhaps over-simplifying the situation. In the UK, among five- to 16-year-old children, Irish travellers and Gypsy/Roma groups are over-represented in experiencing dyslexia, whereas other groups with mixed ethnic backgrounds, or Asian backgrounds, tend to be under-represented. It is difficult to be clear about these learning situations because literacy difficulties may be related to cultural factors for the first group, and to assumptions about language for the second. The high percentage of black Caribbean pupils and mixed white and black Caribbean pupils who are identified as having behavioural, emotional and social difficulties (Lindsay *et al.*, 2006), is also of relevance. It is quite likely that, for some children in this group, their behaviour is masking dyslexia.

Hoyles and Hoyles focus specifically upon the issue of 'missing' dyslexic learners, asking 'Where are the black dyslexics?' (Hoyles and Hoyles, 2007: 8), offering accounts of well-known public figures who experience dyslexia themselves. They raise the issue of other social groups or cultures where dyslexia may be regarded differently, or disregarded. For many of their interviewees, the identification of dyslexia came about as a result of intentional, or accidental, information-gathering of their own. Taken together, these factors remind practitioners to be vigilant for the characteristics of possible dyslexia in all young children.

For practitioners, the most important requirement is that assumptions are not made on the basis of the membership of social, cultural or ethnic groups. The fundamental characteristics of dyslexia will apply equally, and interventions will take a similar form. At this early stage, practitioners may not be discussing possible dyslexia with parents and carers. However, they must take account of parents' and caregivers' concerns, and must find ways of discussing any concerns of their own, in ways that are sensitive to any social, cultural or ethnic considerations. A representative from a local cultural group may be able to support discussions with parents or caregivers if necessary.

Children who are both dyslexic and gifted/talented

Increased understanding of cognitive characteristics has led to the realisation that it is possible to be both gifted or talented in one learning area, and disabled in another. Individuals with this profile are described as having 'dual exceptionality' (Brody and Mills, 1997) or being 'twice exceptional' ('2e'). Morrison and Rizza (2007) believe that this is the hardest group to identify, compared with children who are recognised as gifted and then show a disability later, or with children who are identified as having a specific difficulty or disability and who also have gifts or talents.

Where individuals are both gifted/talented and dyslexic they may exhibit what Dabrowski refers to as 'overexcitability'; this is part of a complex theory of personality development (the Theory of Positive Disintegration) developed by Dabrowski in the 1960s and 1970s. When this is applied to individuals who experience dyslexia (Fischer, 2002), it can describe the state of being in a kind of sensory turmoil, with individuals interested in and stimulated by a wide variety of inputs, making conceptual leaps and new connections, and manifesting shifts of attention. This quality extends to physical activities as well as cognitive ones; individuals may want to be active, on the move and accomplishing things.

Excitability may also look like lack of concentration and attention. A dyslexic learner who is also gifted/talented is likely to find that his or her reading and writing does not keep pace with his or her thinking, and this can cause frustration for children, parents, caregivers and practitioners. It may give rise to a 'mountain goat' effect in written work, as the writer leaps from one topic or point to another. One sentence is on the page and the rest is in the writer's thoughts, making for a disjointed effect that is difficult to overcome because, to the writer, the implications are obvious and it all makes perfect sense.

A child's intelligence or attainment in other areas may mask dyslexia so that he or she appears to be keeping up with their peers, but in fact they are operating at a literacy level below their level of ability. Internally, a child may be experiencing the same dyslexia difficulties as others, such as working harder in order to keep up with peers and, perhaps, producing less; having difficulty in retaining literacy skills; being impeded by fatigue and confusion; and experiencing lack of confidence. A child with this profile might not be recognised as dyslexic and be left to cope alone, with the usual criticisms and accusations of laziness. If their dyslexia has been identified but they are able to keep up with their peers, they may find themselves accused of being fraudulent. These sorts of experiences can have a considerable negative impact and there is a need for counselling, advocacy and literacy support for gifted or talented children who are struggling with dyslexia on their own. Unfortunately, when a learner with this profile is not the child with the greatest need in a class, supporting them may seem inexplicable, or unfair, to others.

Montgomery (2015) considers that children with a 2e profile needs higher-order strategies to help them with their literacy, so that they can use their cognitive strengths to supply knowledge that has not been gained automatically. Strategies would include children exploring the structure of language and literacy, employing the study of linguistics, analysing their own errors and choosing methods to address them. Christian Fischer, researching at the International Center for the Study of Giftedness at the University of Münster, shows that short periods of intervention at a higher level of cognitive demand than usual can also have beneficial effects on literacy skills (Fischer, 2002).

Fischer makes the point that existing systematic phonics programmes for the alleviation of dyslexia are designed for averagely intelligent, rather that gifted, children and may not take account of a gifted child's learning style, causing them frustration and possible distress. However, help for young learners with potential or actual dyslexia who are also gifted or talented, can benefit from dyslexia-aware principles. Pupils with this profile will respond to the kind of teaching and learning that is designed to make input vivid, interesting, meaningful and easier to absorb. Their giftedness makes it possible for them to respond to higher levels of conceptualisation and this must be recognised and explored, otherwise learners may feel under-stimulated and may disengage.

What would dyslexia look like in early childhood?

It is now possible to understand how a very young child may show characteristics that suggest a tendency towards dyslexia. To these should be added family information about reading acquisition and recognition of any strengths and weaknesses, preferences and avoidances in a young child. Finally, in compiling a picture of a young child who may go on to experience dyslexia, parents' concerns must not be overlooked. Very often parents have indications that a child's literacy is not developing in the way that they would expect. Parents' concerns should always be taken seriously, and should help to sharpen focus among practitioners.

Judith Stansfield (2014) points out the similarities between the learning characteristics of a very young child and those of a child experiencing dyslexia; this accords with present-day views of dyslexia as resembling the literacy learning of a younger child. These similarities include difficulties of short-term memory, distractability, letter or number reversals, sequencing issues, difficulties around language and both gross and fine motor skills; she also includes patterns and relationships. Stansfield points out that a child with dyslexia will experience these characteristics for longer, and that they are less easy to overcome. When a family history of dyslexia is added, the possibility of potential dyslexia becomes much clearer.

Dimitra Hartas (2006) suggests that unsettled or negative behaviour could be a possible characteristic of a young child who might go on to develop dyslexia because of links between dyslexia and language. Her concern is that social and emotional interactions and communication are affected by difficulties with expressive and receptive language. A child whose communication is restricted might be seen as lazy or contrary by adults. Other difficulties associated with dyslexia, such as sequencing or following instructions, might also be seen in this way.

These accounts share a difficulty beyond that of recognising potential literacy problems. In each case the discussion spreads out from basic early literacy elements into characteristics that may or may not be part of dyslexia itself, or which may be indicators of other learning characteristics; it depends on how we understand dyslexia. Nevertheless, it is possible to assemble a set of common characteristics that should alert teachers to a possible risk of dyslexia in a young child. Many practitioners consider that they can see learning characteristics that may cause literacy problems later on for a child, but they do not feel able to put these forward until a clearer picture emerges.

Fundamental characteristics of dyslexia for a young child

Language impairment, movement and coordination problems, and also social, emotional and behavioural difficulties, might be telling us about a child's difficulties, but are not, of themselves, indicators of dyslexia. A teacher might reasonably start to wonder about a child's literacy development if they showed any of these characteristics:

- lack interest in books or printed material;
- avoidance of, or reluctance for, literacy-based tasks;
- slow processing of literacy-based tasks;
- avoidance of, or lack of memory for, nursery rhymes and word games;
- extreme difficulty in suggesting a rhyming word;
- extreme difficulty in retrieving the name of an item;
- confusion or immaturity in word choices;
- longer-than-expected time taken to find a word, mentally or on a page;
- immature speech patterns such as short sentences or restricted vocabulary;
- difficulties with repeating a simple rhythmic sequence, tapped or clapped;
- difficulty acquiring or recalling sound or letter knowledge.

It is the persistence over time of difficulties – and their severity, individually or together – that begin to look like warning signs for dyslexia. It would be of particular concern if any of these caused a child distress or resistance, especially if those behaviours were present on a number of occasions. While a child may grow out of some difficulties, it would be wrong to assume that was going to be the case. We expect modern early years practitioners to take notice of situations like these.

Dyslexia-aware principles: what can a practitioner or parent do for young children who might experience dyslexia?

Considerable effort has been put into identifying reliably any incipient signs of dyslexia in young children. However, it is unlikely that many will manifest the significant literacy difficulty that is represented by the term 'dyslexia' to the extent that practitioners feel confident enough to refer concerns to specialists or assessors. At the earliest stages there may be considerable overlap between learning characteristics. Other factors such as life changes, changes of location, relationships and difference in teaching and learning experience may add further complications.

Until difficulty in literacy learning becomes a focus, other features such as sensory characteristics, speech and language or motor control may attract greater concern. For this reason the viability of making recommendations about dyslexia for young children is doubtful. Family information provided by parents or caregivers may add a degree of conviction about the possibility of dyslexia, but this information is not always available, or may itself give rise to difficult issues. Although there may be an early focus upon speech and language, the multi-agency health and wellbeing assessments that are available for young children are unlikely to identify personal characteristics in terms of dyslexia.

A classroom practitioner or parent may feel unsure when it comes to helping young children who are beginning to show signs of struggling with literacy, but the principle of dyslexia awareness can help. Present-day insights identify dyslexia characteristics as resembling those of younger literacy learners and suggest that literacy-related learning for dyslexic learners requires greater intensity (Reid, 2005). The kind of activities that are provided for young children in order to build secure concepts may need to be provided for longer, with concrete apparatus being freely available for as long as children want to use it. In our rush towards meeting scholastic targets, we need not be over-speedy to give up such activities on the grounds that they are too childlike. Instead, we can extend such activities so that they become age-appropriate challenges, encouraging a can-do attitude that helps children to find their own strategies.

Dyslexia-aware practice: put in a step

A dyslexia-aware practitioner, seeing a child struggling to learn a letter or a sound, will think of something to do that would help. A simple but useful principle to remember at this time is that of 'putting in a step' (Pavey, 2013). This can be described as the learning equivalent of a child struggling to climb a doorstep that is too steep; they might manage it if a smaller, temporary step was put in place for them. This individualised learning might not accord with programmes that expect literacy learning to take place at a brisk rate, but may be necessary if learning is to be retained.

To put in a learning step, a practitioner needs to be able to identify the particular small unit learning that is currently presenting a barrier to a child. There needs to be a clear idea of where, in learning terms, a practitioner wants a child to get to and where they are 'now'. A practitioner then thinks of something in between those two points that might help; this could call on creative media. For example, a child who is struggling to remember a letter shape or a sound might remember it better by drawing it, modelling it in clay or some other material, scribing it in a playground by writing with a 'squirty' bottle, matching it to a physical movement, handling it, or drawing or modelling a picture or object to remind themselves of it. Perhaps they might only need help now and again; however, a child who is experiencing possible dyslexia may need a lot of help of this kind, over a long time, and perhaps involving several small steps, plus recall and rehearsal. The thoughts of dyslexia-aware practitioners need to turn automatically to ask and answer the question 'What would be a step in this context?'

Information and communication technology: ICT and young children – perceptions and practices

Electronic ICT devices of various kinds are found in many households and the importance given to these devices continues to increase. Aubrey and Dahl (2014) found that, among their sample of 50 learners aged three to five years, each claimed to have a computer or laptop in their home, although not all of them had internet access.

The range of electronic and communications media devices to which young children have access at home can be considerable. It includes programmable toys, remote controls, cameras, telephones, televisions, DVD players, mobile phones and other platforms and communications devices, including use of Skype. At home, young children may be uploading and downloading materials, taking pictures and making videos, playing games for fun and interacting socially. In learning settings, children are more likely to be using conventional computers with vertical screens, although tablets are becoming more common. Aubrey and Dahl point out the impact of variation in practitioners' perceptions, opinions and expertise regarding ICT, and in the funding available to maintain ICT hardware and software.

A key point to emerge from research in this area is the gap between parents' or carers' and practitioners' understandings of how ICT is used in homes and in early years environments. Research suggests that neither group is really aware how the other group uses ICT with young learners. At times of interaction with parents and caregivers, practitioners tend to inform them about children's skills when using the hardware and software that is available, and about their progress in regard to areas such as literacy and numeracy. This approach assumes that parents and caregivers know about the ICT software and hardware in question.

Observation of children's ICT activity can cast light on how children approach, respond to and use literacy-based ICT input. There is scope for much more useful interaction between homes and early years settings, and this will be helped by increasing the focus upon discussion between parents, carers and practitioners about young children's actual ICT use at home and in early years settings. For children with actual or potential dyslexia, it is often the case that parents, caregivers and grandparents have invested privately in hardware and software to help their children to learn.

Learning game: Grab – supporting sound, letter or word discrimination

This simple game can be used to reinforce sounds, letters, blends or whole words, calling on visual and auditory discrimination. It requires a number of cards prepared in advance, with the target sounds or words shown on them, facing upwards on a table. There are a number of cards for each sound or word. Playing in a small group, children grab the correct cards when a practitioner calls out the target sound or word. If a child grabs the wrong word, they must return all the cards they already hold to the table. The winner is the child holding most cards when the game ends, perhaps after a designated time or number of rounds.

Adapted from McNicholas and McEntee (1991, 2004), no. 29: Word Recognition – Grab (p. 15).

How can dyslexia be supported in this game?

- While it is important to include potentially dyslexic children in groups where there is a range of literacy skills, for this game it would be better to group children at similar levels of literacy, so that one child is not continually disadvantaged and all players have an equal chance to win.

- The game may be played with plastic or wooden letters and blends, for increased multisensory input.
- A practitioner may wish to challenge children by calling a sound or word that only has a small difference to those on the table; for example, he or she may choose to vary a blend slightly, or vary an ending. In this case a dyslexia-aware practitioner will warn players to listen carefully to that part – for example, the second part of a phonic blend, or the ending of a word.

Attitude, understanding, technique and empathy: developing our expertise

Patricia Alexander writes about requirements for both educators and students in the development of expertise. She considers that 'Educators need foundational knowledge, strategies and interests in the academic domains they teach' (Alexander, 2005: 36):

- *attitude*: being interested, personally and professionally, in the areas in which we teach – in this case, early literacy;
- *understanding*: having a foundational knowledge of literacy development and literacy learning;
- *technique*: having a wide range of strategies to counter early literacy difficulty;
- *empathy*: appreciating that being gifted and talented, and dyslexic, can give rise to frustration and anxiety, and that being able to keep pace with one's peers does not mean that there is no dyslexia.

Recommended Reading

1. Hartas, D. (2006) *Dyslexia in the early years*, Abingdon, Routledge
2. Montgomery, D. (2015) *Teaching Gifted Children with Special Educational Needs: Supporting Dual and Multiple Exceptionality* (3rd edn), Abingdon, Routledge
3. Stansfield, J. (2012) *Dyslexia: Early Identification*, Bracknell, British Dyslexia Association, or Stansfield, J. (2014) Early Identification, in J. Carroll and K. Saunders (eds), *The Dyslexia Handbook 2014*, Bracknell, British Dyslexia Association

Useful websites

1. https://www.tes.co.uk/teaching-resources/
   TESconnect is a website for educators and people interested in education. It developed from the *Times Educational Supplement*, which was founded in 1910, swiftly becoming a publication in its own right. Subsequently, it developed into a magazine and now, a website. TESconnect provides materials for early years, primary and other settings. Individuals can access free resources and information, or subscribe to the magazine.
2. http://optimus-education.com/
   Optimus Education offers a free trial of its website, via the early years hub on the home page.
3. http://www.starfall.com/
   Starfall is a website dedicated to children's reading and writing, started in 2002 by Stephen Schutz, who himself experienced literacy difficulty as a child. Materials on the

website are suitable for early childhood and are free, but can be extended by paid membership; the website also has materials for sale.

MY DYSLEXIA EXPERIENCE: I CAN THE SEE THE SIGNS OF DYSLEXIA IN MY SON

My little boy's going to be dyslexic, I know he is, he's just like I was, I can see it. You can't get him to take an interest in books, nursery rhymes, anything like that; he just doesn't want to know. (Parent)

References

Alexander, P. (2005) Teaching Towards Expertise, in P. Tomlinson, J. Dockrell and P. Winne (eds), *Pedagogy: Teaching for Learning*, BJEP Monograph series II, 3, Leicester, British Psychological Society

Aubrey, C. and Dahl, S. (2014) The Confidence and Competence in Information and Communication Technologies of Practitioners, Parents and Young Children in the Early Years Foundation Stage, *Early Years: An International Research Journal*, 34, 1, 94–108

Brody, L. and Mills, C. (1997) Gifted Children with Learning Disabilities: A Review of the Issues, *Journal of Learning Disabilities*, 30, 3, 282–96

Burns, T. and Shadoian-Gersing, V. (2010) *Educating Teachers for Diversity*, Paris, OECD

Fischer, C. (2002) How to Cope with Learning Difficulties of Gifted Children, in F. Mönks and H. Wagner (eds), *Development of Human Potential: Investment into our Future*, Proceedings of the 8th Conference of the European Council for High Ability (ECHA) held in Rhodes, Bonn, European Council for High Ability

Hartas, D. (2006) *Dyslexia in the Early Years*, Abingdon, Routledge

Hoyles, A. and Hoyles, M. (2007) *Dyslexia from a Cultural Perspective*, Hertford, Hansib

Lindsay, G., Pather, S. and Strand, S. (2006) *Special Educational Needs and Ethnicity: Issues of Over- and Under-Representation*, Research Report No. 757, Nottingham, DfES

Lyytinen, H., Erskine, J., Ahonen, T., Aro, M., Ekliund, K., Guttorn, T., Hintikka, S., Hämäläinen, J., Ketonen, R., Laakso, M.-L., Leppänen, P., Lyytinen, P., Poikkeu, A.-M., Puolakanaho, A., Richardson, U., Salmi, P., Tolvanen, A., Torppa, M. and Viholainen, H. (2008) Early Identification and Prevention of Dyslexia: Results from a Prospective Follow-up Study of Children at Familial Risk for Dyslexia, in G. Reid, A. Fawcett, F. Manis and L. Siegel (eds), *The SAGE Handbook of Dyslexia*, London, SAGE

Macdonald, S. (2009) Towards a Social Reality of Dyslexia, *British Journal of Learning Disabilities*, 38, 4, 271–9

McNicholas, J. and McEntee, J. (1991, 2004) *Games to Improve Reading Levels*, NASEN/Routledge

Montgomery, D. (2015) *Teaching Gifted Children with Special Educational Needs: Supporting Dual and Multiple Exceptionality* (3rd edn), Abingdon, Routledge

Morrison, F. and Rizza, M. (2007) Creating a Toolkit for Identifying Twice-Exceptional Students, *Journal for the Education of the Gifted*, 31, 1, 57–76

Pavey, B. (2013) Dyslexia and Creativity, in B. Pavey, M. Meehan and S. Davis, *The Dyslexia-friendly Teacher's Toolkit*, London, SAGE

Raskind, W., Peter, B., Richards, T., Eckert, M. and Berninger, V. (2013) The Genetics of Reading Disabilities: From Phenotypes to Candidate Genes, *Frontiers in Psychology*, 3, article 601, 1–20, available online at: http://www.ncbi.nlm.nih.gov/, accessed 31 May 2014

Reid, G. (2005) Dyslexia, in A. Lewis and B. Norwich (eds), *Special Teaching for Special Children?*, Maidenhead, Open University Press

Scarborough, H. (1989) Prediction of Reading Disability From Familial and Individual Differences, *Journal of Educational Psychology*, 81, 1, 101–8

Shaywitz, S., Fletcher, J., Holahan, J., Schneider, A., Marchione, K., Stuebing, K., Francis, D., Pugh, K. and Shaywitz, B. (1999) Persistence of Dyslexia: The Connecticut Longitudinal Study at Adolecence, *Paediatrics*, 104, 6, 1351–9

Stansfield, J. (2014) Early Identification, in J. Carroll and K. Saunders (eds), *The Dyslexia Handbook 2014*, Bracknell, British Dyslexia Association

Tomlinson, S. (2005) *Education in a Post-Welfare Society* (2nd edn), Open University Press/McGraw-Hill

van der Leij, A., van Bergen, E., van Zuijen, T., de Jong, P., Maurits, N. and Maasen, B. (2013) Precursors of Developmental Dyslexia: An Overview of the Longitudinal Dutch Dyslexia Programme Study, *Dyslexia*, 19, 4, 191–213

Chapter 3

Identifying and assessing dyslexia in the early years

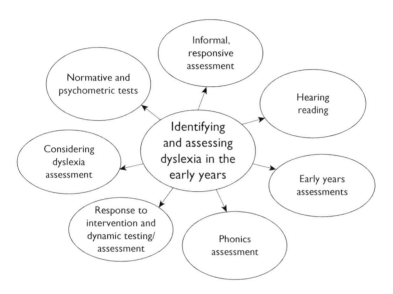

Good practice points

For good practice we need to:

1. hear reading regularly, 'little and often', especially when there are concerns about reading progress;
2. use monitoring and structured observation to gather information when there are concerns about a child's reading;
3. only use a test for the purpose and age range for which it is intended;
4. ensure that any published tests used are up to date;
5. ensure that test procedures are followed correctly by practising test administration beforehand.

Informal, responsive assessment

There may come a point when parents, carers or practitioners begin to feel that a child's early literacy development is not proceeding as expected. There is likely to be a period when a concerned adult considers and explores this possibility. By the time parents or caregivers approach professionals to share their concerns they are likely to have done a considerable amount of thinking and enquiring about the possibility of a literacy difficulty or dyslexia. Riddick (2010) confirms that this is a gradual process, but finds that mothers in her research were able to identify their own children's reading difficulties when they were between the ages of four and seven years.

Formal identification of dyslexia focuses upon a learner's cognitive characteristics, rather than social and environmental aspects. This takes place through norm-based tests, commercially published, which use tightly theorised and designed test items to arrive at a set of scores that show how a child performs in relation to other children. However, before these are employed, it is possible to gain a great deal of understanding about a child's literacy progress through informal assessment methods.

Early years practitioners may feel that they can see the characteristics of developing literacy problems at a very early age, but they may be constrained from mentioning it because a child is very young and is still gaining literacy skills, or because their opinion is not that of a dyslexia specialist or a special educational needs coordinator. Another factor is that a particular child's difficulties may not be the most serious in the group or class, so that lesser concerns may have lower priority. However, parents' intuitions are unlikely to be voiced without good reason, and professionals' intuitions and judgements should also be respected as part of their craft knowledge.

At a fundamental level, a skilled practitioner assesses children all the time. Practitioners in all settings watch how children react, cross-check their own insights and amend their input accordingly. Glynn *et al.* (2006) describe this as 'responsive teaching'. The authors consider that good educational practice includes awareness of the importance of the learning environment and of the scope for interaction with learners; this applies also to non-school settings for young children. A child's reaction and response to input is used to guide practitioners in understanding what a child finds to be difficult, and how best to help them.

In teaching and learning, input needs to be relevant and focused; this is aided when teaching and learning are designed to be dyslexia-accessible, even when discussions of dyslexia are not yet in question. Dyslexia-aware practice is reinforced by a learner's positive response; a practitioner responds to that learning in turn. Responsive teaching, interactive teaching or reciprocal teaching (Palinscar and Brown, 1983) all require a back-and-forth style of teaching and learning, rather than a traditional, transmissive approach. A practitioner is learning from a pupil at the same time as a pupil is learning from a practitioner.

At this level of assessment, where children are very young and just beginning to gain literacy skills, a responsive teacher will be noticing how children react to early literacy activities, songs, rhymes, stories or early books. Difficulty, resistance, or a lack of interest in any of these, or lack of progress when sympathetic methods are used, should make a teacher start to wonder whether a child has met a temporary barrier, or is showing early signs of a greater difficulty.

Hearing reading

Probably the first occasion of assessing a child's literacy comes when adults listen purpose-fully to a child's reading. While the hearing of reading is often carried out by others, in order for a practitioner to know how to help a child they have to listen to reading them-selves. The hearing of reading is generally accompanied by individual teaching, correcting a reader's errors, or asking them to repeat a line, page or book when reading is hesitant. An unknown word can be supported by making it out of letters with a reader, calling on phonemic knowledge, then pointing to it each time it arrives in the text and practising the new word afterwards.

In Pause, Prompt and Praise (Glynn *et al.*, 2006), an adult monitors a child's reading by means of a detailed record. This requires adults, whether practitioners, parents or caregivers, to train themselves to make sure they give a full five seconds of pause before prompting. Prompts follow a specific sequence, providing a framework through which adults can apply precision and consistency in helping a child who is reading to them. Before giving a child a word, the prompts request a child to:

1. read on or read again;
2. think about the meaning of the word;
3. think about the look or sound of the word.

Praise is given if:

1. the word is nearly correct;
2. a child self-corrects without help;
3. a child self-corrects following a tutor's prompt;
4. a child tries hard/works well (Glynn *et al.*, 2006: 148).

When a child is struggling with literacy this approach provides valuable information about how a reading task is tackled and what kind of help is needed. Carried out on a regular basis, the Pause, Prompt and Praise process would provide valuable information about a child's rate of reading progress and any continuing difficulty.

Early years assessments

Young children are already subject to routine health and development checks, which may take place within early childhood settings. With the emphasis on early years education, the carrying out of baseline assessments is often required, setting in place an understanding of the skills a child may bring, or may need, in heading towards primary schooling. Baseline assessments inform measurements of rate of progress; they are not the same as screeners, but may be used for that purpose. A child identified as lagging behind the expected levels of his or her peers would be expected to attract increased educational attention and input in order to improve their skills.

Comparing 28 countries, the Organisation for Economic Cooperation and Development (OECD) confirms that 'Most countries now have national databases on education, and issue educational statistics and indicators. International benchmarking is also increasingly common and is informing national education debates' (OECD, 2013: 2). The OECD indicates that, increasingly, assessment and evaluation are matched directly to learning outcomes, suggesting a potential for learning and teaching to become evaluated in fine detail. This is offset by goals concerning personal and social development within early years assessment systems.

In England, the early years Foundation Stage (EYFS) profile assessment is being replaced by a baseline assessment for children, to be undertaken a few weeks after they enter the Reception class at the age of four or five. This comes into full force in 2016, although schools may adopt it from 2015; until then, the EYFS profile remains in place. The literacy indicators in the EYFS profile for reading and writing are:

- *Reading*: Children read and understand simple sentences. They use phonic knowledge to decode regular words and read them aloud accurately. They also read some common irregular words. They demonstrate an understanding when talking with others about what they have read.
- *Writing*: Children use their phonic knowledge to write words in ways which match their spoken sounds. They also write some irregular common words. They write simple sentences which can be read by themselves and others. Some words are spelled correctly and others are phonetically plausible. (Department for Education and Standards and Testing Agency, 2013: 25)

The Department for Education also maps developmental progress towards these goals; the publication *early years Outcomes* (Department for Education, 2013) offers descriptors from birth to 60 months. Some of the children who cannot meet these reading and writing descriptors are likely to experience potential dyslexia.

Phonics assessment

Teachers generally accept the usefulness of baseline or profile information; more controversial has been the introduction, in England in 2012, of an early years phonics check. This takes place at six years of age and reflects the importance that phonics have come to represent in English literacy learning. The phonics check is a normative test, concerned with identifying whether a child's phonological knowledge and skill is adequate for the level of reading required at the standard age. The check follows a dual route approach to reading acquisition (Castles and Coltheart, 1993) by checking the reading of 20 real words and of 20 non-words. The dual route theory suggests that there are two types of approach to reading print: one where words are recognised by a reader, the other where a reader is able to build unknown words by understanding and reading their phonological components.

It has been pointed out that all unfamiliar words are non-words until a child has learnt to read and attach meaning to them, but the assessment function focuses rather on the listed non-words because it claims that a child cannot possibly have seen these before, and so is forced to try to work them out phonologically. The real words provide a check against this, showing how much more a child might manage when they are reading words that have at least a chance of familiarity. The phonics check is not concerned with identifying dyslexia; nevertheless, the difficulty of phonological skills for the majority of dyslexic learners means that it has meaning for dyslexia-aware practitioners.

Response to Intervention and Dynamic Testing/Assessment

Between informal assessments and formal tests or assessment instruments, there is another approach to assessment that has found relevance for the teaching and learning of literacy, particularly reading. Grigorenko (2009) sees Response to Intervention (RTI) and Dynamic Testing/Assessment (DT/A) as related. RTI is derived from practical operations of teaching and learning, while DT/A has developed from the view that conventional testing is not sufficiently helpful for children with special educational needs and that an alternative, but still rigorous, means of assessment is needed. Both approaches involve teaching the skills or concepts within the assessment. Both approaches may be employed with preschool children.

Dynamic Testing and Assessment involve measuring the rates of progress for a child with special educational needs, with psychological measurement techniques being used to interpret results. Typically, there is a test, an intervention where the learner is taught the required material and then another test to see how much they have improved; this is interpreted as a rate of progress. This process is seen as reflecting more closely an actual learning experience, as it both promotes and assesses the learning; it has been associated with Vygotsky's Zone of Proximal Development.

Response to Intervention is concerned with the learning progress of an individual child. While, in principle, this moves away from a within-child deficit approach, in practice it has settled into a regularised system. The foundation for RTI is the expectation that the majority of children will respond to skilled teaching, so that a child who does not respond by definition needs something further. A child will either 'catch up' and not need further intervention, or will not respond sufficiently and therefore need a higher level of intervention.

There are unresolved issues with this system, since children with dyslexia are unlikely to catch up to the extent that they are performing at the same level as children without dyslexia. There is an issue as to how far successful intervention depends on teachers' personal knowledge and resources. There is a further question as to how far RTI places the responsibility onto the child who does not 'respond', and another as to the consistency of highly skilled, regular teaching. Nevertheless, as a system that focuses on the learning needs of an individual child, that looks at their learning in detail and that offers systematic intervention, practitioners see value in this approach (Grigorenko, 2009; Gorard et al., 2014).

Considering dyslexia assessment

Efforts to identify dyslexic tendencies early have led to the development of normative screening and profiling instruments (see Appendix 1). Screeners and profilers such as these cannot identify dyslexia with certainty without the presence of intractable literacy difficulties. Instead, they identify potentials and tendencies, which help to warn practitioners that there is a serious learning need present, likely to require a focused intervention.

Normative tests, where a child's scores are compared with the scores spread over a population, may be used by teachers to assess literacy. These include tests for reading, spelling, handwriting and reading comprehension. They are designed to assess a child's difficulties, weaknesses, types of errors, persistence and attitudes, and it is difficult to avoid a deficit focus, since a child is tested to the point of failure. Many practitioners have felt uncomfortable subjecting a child to what, for that child, might be a difficult or distressing procedure. For this reason, practitioners have to be careful before deciding to use a test; they should not test more than necessary and they should find ways of encouraging a child and perhaps giving a test in small blocks, without invalidating the test process.

Not all tests are available to practitioners. Some are only available to teachers with a higher qualification; others are only available to qualified psychologists. Practitioners interested in purchasing a test can check its qualification code, or consult the publisher's customer services facility. With a published test, it is particularly important to notice the date of publication; tests may need updating because of obsolete vocabulary and concepts which have dropped out of common usage. It is important to look at the features of the sample of children with whom the test was tried, in its development stage, to make sure that they are appropriate. Tests have to be both valid and reliable: validity means that the test does the job it sets out to do; reliability means that the test does this job in the same way every time it is used. Test manuals contain information about reliability, validity, sample size and test construction, and these should all be considered before purchasing a test.

It should be noted that, for dyslexia assessments of this kind, practitioners have to guard against 'practice effect', also known as 'testing effect'. With over-familiarity, children may remember how to do the test, so that their scores are higher than if they had come to the test without having seen it before. For this reason, practitioners generally should not use a test more frequently than yearly. Tests may also be published with two different forms, to safeguard against children remembering the test items. Further information about assessments for dyslexia can be found in Appendix 1.

Normative and psychometric tests

Psychometric tests, literally measuring the psyche or mind, have figured largely in dyslexia assessment. This is because an early way of identifying dyslexia was to look for a pattern that showed high levels in most areas, but with a noticeable dip in reading and spelling, possibly with associated difficulties in other aspects like sequencing or memory. In some assessments the size of this gap between literacy and other attainment was measured, and if it was of a sufficiently large size it was considered to confirm an identification of dyslexia. This discrepancy model, as it was known, is no longer used to assess dyslexia, since we no longer think of dyslexia as the province of highly intelligent children with an unexplained inability to gain literacy skills. Nevertheless, seeing a notable difference between literacy and other functioning is still the ultimate identifier for dyslexia.

All assessments can give false positives and false negatives, identifying issues where there are none, or failing to identify issues when they are actually present. A practitioner needs to bear this in mind, keeping a watch on a child's progress and respecting instincts which suggest that there might be a difficulty. Different tests do different jobs, and they do them in different ways. It is important for practitioners to know which assessments to use for which purpose, and why. Most countries publish codes of practice, often through professional psychological associations, and these provide guidance in the ethical use of assessments. Also, firms specialising in test publishing have members of staff who will provide helpful advice.

Normative and psychometric tests provide information by comparing a child's performance with others of the same age. The results from these tests are expressed as a 'raw scores', which are then converted to standardised scores. The latter term refers to a calculation by which all test scores are turned into levels where they may be compared with each other. This is helpful when there are several tests involved, such as when a child's different literacy skills are assessed. It then becomes possible to see where a child's relative strengths and weaknesses might lie, and to consider whether their learning profile is characteristic of dyslexia.

Normative and psychometric tests can assess a child's literacy in this way, but some psychometric assessments are used to provide a wider view of a child's cognitive skill. They look at the range of a child's potential and/or performance in a number of areas in order to gain understanding of aspects of cognition such as knowledge and understanding, information-processing, problem-solving and skill speed. Within this range of characteristics, weaknesses that are associated with literacy difficulty may be identified. Whether assessments are carried out by specialist teachers or by psychologists, they will generally include elements that allow for an understanding of a child's overall abilities. If there are significant literacy-related difficulties visible among the subtests, this might support a conclusion that a child's difficulties are dyslexic in nature.

Although a considerable number of tests have been published, when it comes to assessment for very young children, the 2013 guide from the New Zealand Psychologist's Board warns that a number of sources should be used when gathering information about their literacy. The guide points out that, for a number of reasons, it is very difficult to capture the real experience of young children's behaviour using a formal assessment instrument. The guide continues, 'If the purpose of the assessment is to develop an intervention plan, other assessment methods such as direct observation in natural settings and structured interviews should be used' (New Zealand Psychologists Board, 2013: 22).

There are many published assessment instruments or tests designed to arrive at a set of scores that show how a child performs in relation to other children. Trained practitioners may use many of these but they are more likely to be the responsibility of a special educational needs or dyslexia specialist. Dyslexia assessment often takes place because a parent or caregiver is worried about a child's literacy progress. In the first instance, any such family concerns should be raised with a child's school or setting. If concerns continue after informal and specialist teacher assessment, further consultation might involve an educational psychologist, paediatrician, or speech and language therapist.

Dyslexia-aware principles: observation

Observations are now a part of a practitioner's regular work, being required for the recording of teaching and learning moments that might be quite fleeting. There are many factors to consider in observation, and there are ways to make an observation more effective and powerful. In the context of dyslexia and young children, hopefully a practitioner would notice early literacy activities that are not developing as expected. At that time they may wish to undertake a more systematic observation.

Denscombe (2010: 200) points out that systematic observations can cover:

- how often events occur;
- what is happening at a given time;
- how long events last for;
- what is taking place with a particular individual or group of individuals.

There are also disadvantages, which include the fact that an observation will provide information about behaviour or events but not the reasons for them. Furthermore, an observation may over-simplify, since it is not likely to explore a deeper understanding of behaviour or events. An observation is unlikely to provide information about settings or contexts and, finally, the presence of the observer may affect the behaviour or events being observed. There are ethical implications for observation, and covert observation may now be seen as dubious, since it takes place without the 'subject's' consent. Ethical practice is best followed by seeking the permission of parents/carers and the headteacher, if a structured observation is planned.

In arranging an observation there are techniques that can provide practitioners with more information than just watching a child and noting down what they do, which is a practice that may, in problematic situations, focus too much upon negatives. Observers, too, may demonstrate bias in observation or interpretation. It might be best to have two observers, but this would be very difficult to do in a busy school or nursery. Structured, systematic observations offer some protection against this, and Kate Wall offers a number of possibilities:

- *time sampling*: when an activity or behaviour is noted at pre-decided times within a certain time-frame;
- *event or frequency sampling*: when a practitioner seeks to record how often something takes place;
- *focused or targeted child observations*: when detailed notes are made regarding the child's actions or behaviour at a specific, previously decided time;
- *sociograms*: when a practitioner seeks to establish and quantify a child's social relationships, actions or communications;
- *movement*: when a practitioner seeks to establish a child's choices of activity and their movement between activities. (Wall, 2006: 112–19)

Dyslexia-friendly practice: movement observation

Appendix 2 is adapted from Kate Wall's (2006) diagram showing a movement-tracking chart, with the addition of the time spent at each activity and a note showing whether it was instigated by a teaching assistant. A practitioner seeking to do an observation of this kind would need to prepare the plan of locations beforehand. The example in Appendix 2 shows a child who is avoiding the book corner; this might suggest to a practitioner that further investigation could be useful.

Denscombe (2010) mentions the difficulty of putting into context the information from an observation. Appendix 3 provides a photocopiable template that allows for the recording of contextual information by noting not only what a child or group is doing at any given time, but also what the teacher, the teaching assistant and the other children are doing. Experience shows that it is possible to complete such a sheet at 2.5-minute intervals. Denscombe makes the point that an observation needs to be supported with field notes to provide context and detail, and the template includes a reminder of this.

Information and communication technology: three established literacy programs which include assessment of progress

Many of the computer-based activities aimed at helping reading and spelling will include measures of progress so that a child can try to improve their scores. Three well-known programs for developing literacy are shown here; they all include assessment records within their structure. These programs are available for use at home, as well as being used in schools.

1. **RocketReader** (published by RocketReader Online) is a program that develops speed of reading, vocabulary and comprehension. It is suitable for learners from the age of five onwards. A free trial is available at: http://www.rocketreader.com/
2. **Wordshark** (published by Whitespace Central) has been the most commonly used British program for helping learners who experience dyslexia. It offers games for reading and spelling, and reward activities. It is generally used by learners from the age of five onwards. Online tutorials are available at: http://www.wordshark.net/
3. **Successmaker** (published by Pearson Global Schools) is a program developed in the USA, covering literacy, language, mathematics and learning management. It is suitable for children from the age of five onwards. A free demonstration is available at: http://www.pearsonglobalschools.com/

Learning game: Guess the Sound or Letter – supporting sound and letter discrimination

This game calls on tactile sense, and asks a child to think about identifying something they cannot see. A three-dimensional letter (made of plastic, wood or strong card) is placed in an opaque bag, or placed in a child's hands when their eyes are shut. The aim is to guess the sound, or the letter; a child who guesses correctly keeps the letter for the duration of the game. If a letter is not correctly guessed, it goes back into the store for identification. When the game has finished, children can be invited to make something with the letters they hold, such as a shape, tower or chain, or to draw round them, or to draw a picture using their letter shape(s).

Adapted from McNicholas and McEntee (1991, 2004), no. 17: Letter Recognition – Guess the Letter (p. 10).

How can dyslexia be supported in this game?

- A practitioner needs to give a clear instruction as to whether he or she is looking for letter sounds or letter names.
- Similarly, a practitioner needs to decide, and make clear, whether the game will be played with capitals, lower-case letters, or a combination of both.
- The game can be steered by restricting it to a chosen selection of sounds or letters.
- A potentially dyslexic child can be given practice beforehand, bearing in mind that learners with dyslexia often do not remember easily.
- A potentially dyslexic child who has the job of placing the letters in the bag or in another child's hands has more time to think about the sound/letter in question. They need not have this job every time, but being the chooser, sometimes, means that they are not always at a disadvantage.
- Making a shape or picture from the letter reinforces its identification while not relying on literacy skill.

Attitude, understanding, technique, empathy: the assessment of dyslexia

The purpose of dyslexia-related assessment is to help a child to gain literacy skills. An appropriate assessment stance follows from this:

- *attitude*: believing that teacher's judgement is valuable, so that formal tests are not too heavily relied upon, and formal testing is not carried out too often;
- *understanding*: knowing that all tests contain a certain level of error, in addition to any human error that may creep in, and psychometric tests can show false positives or false negatives;
- *technique*: being able to apply a full range of informal assessments, including structured observation, in seeking to be able to understand and aid a child's learning;
- *empathy*: considering how negative an experience it might be to be tested, especially for a child with literacy difficulties.

Recommended reading

1. Backhouse, G. and Ruback, P. (2011) *Special Needs Language and Literacy Assessment Handbook for Primary and Secondary Schools*, London, Hodder Education. Includes photocopiable resources
2. Phillips, S., Kelly, K. and Symes, L. (2013) *Assessment of Learners with Dyslexic-Type Difficulties*, London, SAGE
3. Wall, K. (2006) *Special Needs and Early Years* (2nd edn), London, SAGE

Useful websites

1. http://wwwsasc.org.uk
   The SpLD Assessment Committee oversees all matters concerning the assessment of dyslexia and other specific learning difficulties (SpLD).

2. http://www.nhs.uk
    The NHS Choices Dyslexia – Diagnosis page offers helpful advice to parents as to how to go about sharing concerns regarding dyslexia, whom to consult and, if matters are not resolved, how to seek an in-depth assessment.
3. http://www.dyslexiaaction.org.uk
    There are many organisations and individuals offering purchasable, independent dyslexia assessments. Dyslexia Action is an organisation with longstanding experience, expertise and high reputation in this area.

MY DYSLEXIA EXPERIENCE: MY OWN DYSLEXIA ASSESSMENT

I was assessed for dyslexia, and I couldn't help thinking how sad it was that we put children through this. It took ages, it was exhausting and it focused on all the things I couldn't do. My dyslexia wasn't recognised when I was at school; I hope we can do better nowadays. (Dyslexic practitioner)

References

Backhouse, G. and Ruback, P. (2011) *Special Needs Language and Literacy Assessment Handbook for Primary and Secondary Schools*, London, Hodder Education

Castles, A. and Coltheart, M. (1993) Varieties of Developmental Dyslexia, *Cognition*, 47, 2, 149–80

Denscombe, M. (2010) *The Good Research Guide* (4th edn), Maidenhead, Open University Press/McGraw-Hill

Department for Education (2013) *Early Years Outcomes*, London, DfE, available online at: https://www.gov.uk/

Department for Education and Standards and Testing Agency (2013) *Early Years Foundation Stage Profile*, London, DfE, available online at: https://www.gov.uk/

Glynn, T., Wearmouth, J. and Berryman, M. (2006) *Supporting Students with Literacy Difficulties: A Responsive Approach*, Maidenhead, Open University Press

Gorard, S., Siddiqui, N. and See, B. H. (2014) *Response to Intervention Evaluation Report and Executive Summary*, London, Education Endowment Foundation

Grigorenko, E. (2009) Dynamic Assessment and Response to Intervention: Two Sides of One Coin, *Journal of Learning Disabilities*, 42, 2, 111–32

McNicholas, J. and McEntee, J. (1991, 2004) *Games to Improve Reading Levels*, NASEN/Routledge

New Zealand Psychologists Board (2013) *Guidelines on the Use of Psychometric Tests*, available online at: http://www.psychologistsboard.org.nz/

Organisation for Economic Cooperation and Development (OECD) (2013) *Synergies for Better Learning: an International Perspective on Evaluation and Assessment* (Summary), OECD Reviews of Evaluation and Assessment in Education, Paris, OECD

Palinscar, A. and Brown, A. (1983) *Reciprocal Teaching of Comprehension-monitoring Activities*, Technical Report No. 269, Champaign, University of Illinois

Riddick, B. (2010) *Living with Dyslexia* (2nd edn), Abingdon, David Fulton/Routledge

Wall, K. (2006) *Special Needs and Early Years* (2nd edn), London, SAGE

Chapter 4

The emotional impact of dyslexia

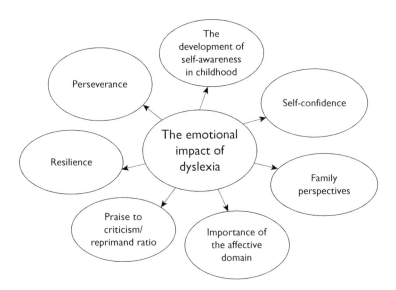

The development of self-awareness in childhood

Perseverance

Self-confidence

The emotional impact of dyslexia

Resilience

Family perspectives

Praise to criticism/ reprimand ratio

Importance of the affective domain

Good practice points

For good practice we need to:

1. perform a mental check to ensure that we remember the importance of the affective domain;
2. avoid blaming or criticising children when they have difficulty in literacy or are reluctant to engage with it;
3. seek to improve our praise to criticism/reprimand ratio;
4. help children to develop resilience and perseverance in the face of literacy difficulties by offering them the chance to shine in other areas;
5. avoid exposing children with literacy difficulties to embarrassment by asking them to read, write or spell in front of others, instead making these voluntary.

The development of self-awareness in childhood

The development of self-awareness or self-concept in young children is an area of consider-able research in child psychology. Self-awareness is generally thought to develop at around 18 months to two years, as shown by a child being able to recognise themselves in a mirror (Rochat, 2003). By the age of two they have a sense of 'me' (themselves) and at around five years of age children recognise themselves, not only from their own vantage point but also from the point of view of others. Rochat believes that this is the point at which children start evaluating themselves. A 'self-conscious' view of a child's own self can give rise to positive and negative feelings, such as embarrassment, 'pride or shame' (op.cit. 722). These are feel-ings that exist in relation to others.

One aspect of children's developing ideas about themselves is 'academic self-concept'. This is one of a number of ideas that we have about ourselves – in this case, concerning how skilled we are in academic matters. We can imagine this arising as we start to evaluate our-selves against others. Some researchers see it as an early development, influenced by parents' views, while others link academic self-concept to the quality of relationships with teachers and, to some extent, with mothers (Verschueren *et al.*, 2012).

Academic self-concept is linked to self-esteem; this has been explored in relationship to children who experience dyslexia. However, Burden (2008) warns against making too simple an association of cause and effect between literacy difficulty and self-esteem. The impact of dyslexia relates to how important literacy is in a person's life, and for some people it may not be important at all. Nevertheless, the demands of literacy are often culturally significant and, under such demands, it is possible to sense that a young child may start to develop doubts about their own literacy skills at a very early age.

This is a deeply complex area of child development and one that has psychological, social, philosophical and educational aspects. Burden warns us that this, too, must not be over-simplied as our ideas about ourselves relate to our sense of identity, our sense of self-efficacy and to the roles, influences and powers that we attribute to other people. Views about the development of self are by no means agreed, the relationship of these views to each other is not agreed and, at this stage, there may not be a secure basis for measurement. Nevertheless, a sense of identity is important and this is affected by a person's dyslexia experience.

Self-confidence

Away from the strictness of psychological concepts, the impact of dyslexia is often discussed in terms of bringing about a lack of confidence in learners. Lack of confidence in this case suggests a combination of puzzlement, anxiety, fear, self-doubt and lack of self-esteem. However, if the impact that dyslexia has upon a learner's confidence is more widely recog-nised today, so too is the understanding that much can be achieved when students are encouraged and their confidence supported. Burden confirms that self-esteem can change for the better as dyslexic individuals become older.

Confidence comes from success, so a range of opportunities is needed which will both pro-mote success in literacy learning and put a 'safety net' under young learners at possible risk of dyslexia. We need to help children who might be dyslexic to move from a position of uncertainty, doubt or resistance to one of resilience and perseverance. As children grow up in a climate where dyslexia is understood, and adjustments are made, it is to be hoped that schooling may become more of a positive experience than it was for previous generations. Younger learners are only just starting their journey to literacy and we can aim to minimise the development of poor confidence and lack of self-esteem through sensitive, careful and focused teaching.

Family perspectives

There are a number of aspects of family life that can change when a child experiences dyslexia. Family relationships may include interactions with parents, caregivers, grandparents, siblings and extended family members, and there may be a wealth of experience, opinion and belief in conversations about dyslexia. A confirmation of dyslexia is likely to come later in a child's schooling, when difficulties with formal reading and spelling begin to cause concern.

There is continuing debate about whether or not a 'label' of dyslexia is helpful. For many parents and carers, having a named identification helps in their understanding of aspects of their child's development that have been puzzling them, and helps them to identify ways to assist and support literacy learning. For a child, it may help their sense of identity as a person who can be effective in other ways; typically, a child may have feared that they were 'thick' and may have been tormented or bullied for this reason.

It should not be forgotten that parents may be dyslexic themselves; this can give rise to complexity in family dynamics (Scott, 2004). Dyslexic parents may feel that it is difficult for them to help their children in the way a school wants them to; schools expect certain kinds of support for schoolwork, yet for some family members this simply might not be possible. Parents may feel ambivalent about school interactions when remembering their own schooling, or they may feel frustrated at how, or whether, schools are helping their child.

At the early years stage there is unlikely to be an identification of dyslexia unless an early screening has been carried out, and screening only identifies possibility. The issues for educators focus on concerns that arise when a child is not making the expected progress in literacy tasks. However, for parents, the process and the issues may be different. Parents may compare their children with others in their family, noticing developmental differences. They may identify characteristics that they have experienced themselves, or that they have seen in other family members. Nursery rhymes and stories may not attract a child's interest, and parents may notice developmental characteristics such as late talking, or clumsiness, which later seem relevant in an identification of dyslexia. While they may not always have known the reason for the difficulty, some mothers in Barbara Riddick's (2010) research describe changes in their children's emotional response to school once formal literacy learning began. Their children became withdrawn, depressed, anxious or resistant, whereas previously they had not shown these characteristics.

The importance of the affective domain

Present-day learning theory, including dyslexia theory, may focus on personal factors, environmental factors, or factors of practice. Within the personal factors, discussion can highlight a cognitive domain as a territory which covers intellectual development, and an affective domain which covers feelings, emotions and responses. These ideas have proved long-lasting, providing a framework for thinking about the areas of knowledge and emotion. However, the areas are not totally separate – there is considerable overlap between them and making too sharp a distinction between them is unhelpful (Bloom *et al.*, 1964/1973).

The importance of the affective/emotional area in teaching and learning is recognised; the Rose Report (Rose, 2009) points out its importance in gaining literacy skills. Bloom and his co-authors identified an important insight about this aspect of teaching and learning; they found that there was a tendency for erosion, over time, of the affective elements in educational programmes. That is to say, practitioners start by taking care of feelings, by noticing emotional impact, by taking it into account and by engaging learners. However, with familiarity this becomes pared away until only the 'bare bones' of the cognitive knowledge remain. Learning may then be less effective, but the practitioner does not know why, since, in terms of content, they are still doing what they usually do. In order to counter this tendency and keep our input fresh, we need to review our own practice regularly, ensuring that affective aspects are always considered and included.

Praise to criticism/reprimand ratio

The idea of praise as a way to improve motivation goes back a long way, but is quantified in Flora's (2000) focus on the five-to-one praise ratio, drawing on earlier research. This suggests that an instance of criticism needs five instances of praise to have the same level of impact. The same goes for reprimands; negative judgements hit us harder. The actual ratio of praise to criticism or reprimand may vary according to sources, but there is strong support for the view that individuals need more praise to counteract negative effects. For some people this is not a worthy strategy; they may say that learners should not be praised merely for doing what they are supposed to do. However, Flora traces the link between approval and the reinforcing of desired behaviour. If we are trying to help a small child to persevere and develop confidence in the face of a significant struggle with early literacy activities, praise is more likely to generate the resilience needed.

Flora set his students the task of monitoring their own approval-to-disapproval ratio. They picked a particular time, for an hour a day, over seven days, in order to find their baseline for giving praise and criticism. Using the same time and duration, they then tried to improve their practice over roughly ten days, to the point where they were giving five items of praise to one of criticism.

We can monitor our own approval-to-disapproval ratio in the same way; Appendix 4 provides a chart to support this process. During praise and criticism events we can make a simple 'check' mark to count instances, but for more information we can note any behaviour changes and any other circumstances that may have brought about the change apart from our own approval and disapproval. This chart would need to be copied and used twice; once for a baseline and once for our efforts to improve our ratio. It should be noted that we would undertake this monitoring in order to improve our own practices, rather than a child's. If we want to try to improve a child's behaviour through monitoring of this sort, ethical practice requires that we discuss it with the headteacher and parents first.

It takes a deliberate intention to build up our praise level when interacting with children who are not engaging with literacy. At times it may be very difficult to get a child's cooperation and there may be extreme reactions, so that praise seems out of the question. Furthermore, we may think we are praising a child frequently and regularly, yet somehow those words remain unsaid and what is spoken aloud is criticism or reprimand. Nevertheless, it is worth making the effort to find things to praise if it secures a child's confidence. Teaching need not always confront the most difficult challenges head-on; praise for other aspects and achievements can lighten the mood, creating a kinder atmosphere and helping a child to persevere.

Zentall and Morris (2012) go further, exploring the view that the kind of praise given has an impact upon motivation. Praise needs to be specific, and directed personally at the child. To tell a child that they are a good reader is to tell them only that they are one of a group, some of whom may be better at reading than they are. This may create anxiety or negativity, and a focus upon error; what is needed is to tell the child that they, themselves, read well, or that they have done their reading task well. Praise needs to be varied and not only verbal; gesture and expression can also demonstrate praise. Some disapproval is still appropriate and it provides a contrast, but is likely to occur naturally. As for frequency of praise, following Rawson's 1992 research, Flora recommends three praise events each day, in the context of his own research. This takes practice, but, as a bonus, Flora reports that 'When the behavior of one child is praised, teachers and parents often find that other children then imitate the behavior' (Flora, 2000: 67).

Resilience

Discussions of resilience or resiliency focus upon children who are at considerable risk of adverse social situations, of a kind that might threaten not only their wellbeing but their very lives. Resilience describes the quality of being able to recover quickly, overcoming adverse situations and growing up into coping, well-balanced adults. While literacy difficulty may not be of the same magnitude as situations like these, there is no doubt about its impact. Resilience is needed to find the perseverance to overcome literacy difficulty and to allow other qualities to come forward helping a child to build a positive identity.

Not all people who experience dyslexia are undermined by it. Some people will take pride in their accomplishments, and in the alternative perspectives and approaches that dyslexia may give them. Following the social model of disability, some people will insist on the right to their own dyslexic style of reading, writing and spelling, seeing it as just one part of the range of universal human experience – this view is one of dyslexia pride. Whether or not they come to take this view later in life, for very young children at the start of their literacy development it is important to help them to build resilience. Benard's work in developing the resilience of children shows that it is never too early to start. She states that 'Resilient children are considerably more responsive (and can elicit more response from others), more active, and more flexible and adaptable even in infancy' (Benard, 1991: 7). This suggests that it would be useful for even very young children to be encouraged to respond and communicate, cope with change and adapt to circumstances.

Factors that build resilience in young people are support, high expectations, encouragement and participation, in schools, families and communities. Benard describes the characteristics of children's resilience as social competence, problem-solving skills, autonomy (independence) and sense of purpose and future (ibid.: 9), qualities that are located strongly in the affective domain. Bearing in mind that these ideas are focused upon children with high levels of risk in their lives, they still have relevance for children who are experiencing literacy difficulty and who will continue to experience it throughout their school careers. Benard considers that a positive school experience, including well-founded teaching and learning programmes, can alter the dynamics for a child so that they can become more resilient.

Perseverance

There is no doubt that a child who experiences dyslexia has to work hard to overcome it. This can give rise to the view that hard work is the deciding factor and therefore a child with literacy difficulty must not be working hard enough. Such a view is unfair; not only does it overlook the fatigue factor, the truth, also, is that working harder at something that is not being effective will not help. It is the responsibility of educators to find the things that will help, and to direct a child's efforts towards these.

Nevertheless, we should not be afraid to encourage children to work hard and persevere, as long as we do it kindly and give praise for the effort. There is more chance for perseverance and success if tasks are differentiated and tailored to include work that a child can manage, together with work that stretches them a little, but not too much. In a busy classroom with a tightly designed curriculum it is difficult to take time to improve work, but human beings do, after all, improve their skills with practice. There is a place to ask even young children to 'have another go' and see if they can do the work better – we can ask this as long as we do it kindly and praise the effort. It is possible to say, even to young children 'See what you can do, see if you can do it better this time. What do you think could be made better? Would you like to have another try?', aiming to take the emotional stress out of the situation and making it more game-like. If the work is produced twice, a child can then decide which one is better, and why.

Dyslexia-aware principles: the place of the affective domain in early years settings

The interest in early years education is now global. It is included within the United Nations Millennium Development Goals of 2000, which address the purposes of eradicating poverty and hunger, and implementing universal primary education. early years and preschool provision is linked to this through the UNESCO Education for All first goal: 'expand early childhood care and education'. This goal is intended to be met by 2015, but is likely to be a work in progress for some members. In a presentation for the United Nations Children's Fund (UNICEF), Zafeirakou makes the point that 'The quality of interactions between the teacher and the child is the single most important determinant of programme success' (Zafeirakou, 2012: slide 29). While good-quality interactions will include clear, skilled and knowledgeable teaching, they must also include attention to the affective domain and the development of social and emotional skills.

The nature of both cognitive and affective interactions in early years or preschool provision depends on the age range involved, and this in turn is governed by the age at which formal schooling begins. For UNESCO it is from birth to eight years, for Zafeirakou it is birth to six to eight years; individual countries' early years provision may begin at two or three years. Some countries begin formal schooling at six years of age, others at seven; in the UK it is five; the early years Foundation Stage runs from birth to five years. early years or preschool frameworks inevitably contain a social-emotional element or ethos. Whatever may be a nation's time-frame for early years and preschool provision, the requirement for practitioners to understand, and work towards, children's social, emotional and cognitive development is consistent. This becomes even more critical when children are at risk of losing confidence and morale through potential or actual dyslexia.

Dyslexia-aware practice: process, product and the affective domain

We can think of early years practice as encompassing both process and product. These would roughly correspond to the affective and cognitive domains of learning, and to the dual aims of early years provision: development for life, and preparation for early schooling. If 'product' describes curricular content, then 'process' describes thinking about how we undertake our teaching and learning – our pedagogy. The two elements need to balance, and since the affective domain is prone to erosion, we need to remind ourselves to include affective elements. Teaching and learning go much better when these are remembered. Before beginning teaching we can perform a mental check, asking ourselves:

- Are our pupils hungry, tired, fearful, upset, or worried about anything *outside* the classroom?
- Are our pupils worried about anything *inside* the classroom?
- Does our teaching include something that will engage children's personal attention and interest?
- Have we thought about the emotional impact of the content that we are teaching?
- Can we use humour ourselves, and encourage humour in children, to keep the mood light and minimise stress?
- Do we make sure to spare children pain and embarrassment in early reading, spelling and writing activities?
- What shall we do if a child reacts emotionally to our teaching: do we have a backup plan?

Information and communication technology: mobile platforms – tablets, smart phones and application programmes (apps)

The nature of ICT has changed in recent years, with the introduction of mobile devices such as tablets and smart phones. Purchasers install their own choice of application programs (apps). Some of these are free, perhaps carrying advertisements, while others have a relatively small cost, although for some apps the initial, minimal cost can lead purchasers to much more expensive functions. The availability of apps depends on the operating system, and the two main systems currently available are Apple Inc.'s 'i' Operating System (iOS) and Android, developed by Google. At the time of writing the iOS has the major share of the market through its iPads® and iPhones®. Correspondingly, the iOS currently has the majority of apps, although some apps are available for both systems. There are other mobile platforms available; some apps will run on personal computers and laptops. Apps are obtained through online 'stores', including those operated by Apple, Google, Google Chrome and Samsung, and these show examples and free trials.

Many apps are designed for young children, either as games or as educational content; often they are both. While some may suggest a starting age of three or four years, parents report children as young as two having their own mobile devices and favourite software; some apps are aimed at children of this age. Young children can operate touch screens more easily than keyboards and they are attracted by good visual displays, entertainment value and familiarity through parents' or carers' usage. Increasingly, schools are employing mobile technology for its educational potential. These are used for individual activities, for opportunities to upload and download materials or scripts and for linking with large electronic white boards or projectors in classrooms.

The fine motor control required by touch screens, and the shape matching required by puzzles and games, are bound to help young children to gain manipulative skills and visual discrimination abilities. However, when it comes to literacy, guidelines that apply to print text also apply to apps. While there are many apps that focus on early literacy activities, a great many employ upper case letters. Young children generally learn Roman alphabet letters as lower case first, so this kind of alphabet is preferred. Also, for a child who may experience potential or actual dyslexia, cluttered screens or over-active animations will not help. Bearing in mind that new apps are being developed all the time, the *Guardian* newspaper publishes internet lists of 50 best apps for children (www.theguardian.com); other internet lists of apps for children are also available.

Learning games: Change Places; King or Queen of the Circle – mixing children and supporting sound, letter or blend discrimination

These games are developed from a useful game for mixing a larger group of people; it is particularly valuable when they do not know each other – for example, when children join a new class. It can start simply and increase its demand as literacy skills increase. If any children do not want to play, they can be allowed to sit out and watch, and encouraged to join in another time.

1. Everyone forms a circle, including a practitioner. The practitioner calls out instructions like 'Change places … if you are wearing something blue' or '… if you have brown hair' or '… if you have white socks' and so on. Children check themselves, and swap places in the circle. The practitioner makes sure to include him or herself in at least one of the swaps.
2. Children each have a card with a sound/letter on it; there are a number of cards for each sound/letter; the teacher has a larger set, containing the same sound/letters. The teacher holds up a card and says 'Change places … if you have one like this,' waiting until the right children have moved and everyone has settled before he or she proceeds (speed can be increased later).
3. A practitioner adds a sound element, while holding up the card: 's … Change places if you have s' and so on. This can be used for whatever sounds/letters or blends the practitioner wants children to learn. After a while, a practitioner no longer needs to tell children to change places; he or she may just call out the sound/letter or blend.

4. At a more complex level, a fun element of challenge is introduced. A child stands in the middle; when the teacher calls out the sound/letter or blend the child in the middle tries to run into a vacant space while all the others run to change places. The remaining child without a space goes to the middle. This child will still have a letter/sound or blend of their own, so the practitioner will need to make it plain that they can run to a space whatever sound is called. They can be named King or Queen of the Circle in order to reinforce this, and to remove any anxiety that may come from being last to find a place.

5. At the game's most developed level, a practitioner calls out a word beginning with the sound/letter or blend, without using cards; the children change places and the King or Queen of the Circle tries to get into a vacant space, as before.

Adapted from McNicholas and McEntee (1991, 2004), no. 42: Blends – Change the Circle (p. 26).

How can dyslexia be supported in these games?

*   Familiarity with the game is built slowly, so that a potentially dyslexic child is not trying to manage new instructions and new literacy demands – in the form of sounds, letters, or blends – at the same time.
*   The games teach the desired sound/letter or blend in multisensory ways, calling on visual, auditory and kinaesthetic senses, and gross motor skills. This is recognised as good practice for teaching learners who experience dyslexia or possible dyslexia.
*   The game offers a different and fun way of reinforcing sounds/letters or blends introduced previously.
*   Within the game, a practitioner can prompt a child who looks as though they are not going to change places at the right time. If they become King or Queen of the Circle by being last, they are likely to find a vacant place on the next round, and the game moves on.
*   Slower response to the target sound might be due to speed of processing rather than lack of sound/letter recognition. A dyslexia-aware practitioner may investigate this for themselves, thinking about what it may imply for other literacy tasks.

Attitude, understanding, technique, empathy: maintaining the affective domain

As practitioners, we need to be vigilant that we do not let the affective domain erode in our teaching, thereby reducing our effectiveness. Attitude, understanding, technique and empathy in this context include:

*   *attitude*: accepting the importance of the affective domain and of not allowing affective elements to erode in our pedagogy;
*   *understanding*: expecting that children who experience possible or actual dyslexia can make progress and can improve their work, with supportive approaches;
*   *technique*: improving our praise to criticism/reprimand ratio;
*   *empathy*: recognising the impact of dyslexia upon a learner's confidence and finding helpful ways to encourage that confidence.

Recommended reading

1. Flora, S. (2000) Praise's Magic Reinforcement Ratio: Five to One Gets the Job Done, *The Behaviour Analyst Today*, 1, 4, 62–9
2. Riddick, B. (2010) *Living with Dyslexia* (2nd edn), Abingdon, David Fulton/Routledge
3. Scott, R. (2004) *Dyslexia and Counselling*, London, Whurr

Useful websites

1. http://www.dystalk.com
   This website has many useful video talks. To see Professor Amanda Kirby talk about self-esteem, go to early years and Preschool in the left-hand menu.
2. http://www.schoolsworld.tv
   SchoolsWorld developed from Teacher's TV and includes many interesting and useful early years items. Searching on 'Dyslexia' accesses a video about developing self-esteem in dyslexic children.
3. http://www.theschoolrun.com
   TheSchoolRun is a UK website run by mothers of schoolchildren. The website offers free materials and suggestions for Reception-age children (five years) and older.

MY DYSLEXIA EXPERIENCE: TEACHERS KNOW BETTER NOW

As a child it was very difficult for me. My parents were very academic and teachers couldn't believe that I might not be. They would probably say they were just being firm and encouraging … but, looking back, I would say they bullied me, they told me off in front of everyone. My parents say that they wish now they had done more for me, but they didn't know any better. Eventually they got me a tutor. You can bet I would go to battle for my son, he's dyslexic too, he corrects me sometimes, he's better than me at some things. Teachers know more about dyslexia now and if my son got one who didn't, or who denied it, you can bet I would make a fuss about it. (Dyslexic parent)

References

Benard, B. (1991) *Fostering Resiliency in Kids? Protective Factors in the Family, School and Community*, Washington, DC, Western Regional Center for Drug-free Schools and Communities, Department of Education

Bloom, B., Krathwohl, D. and Masia, B. (eds) (1964/1973) *Taxonomy of Educational Objectives Book 2*, London, Longman

Burden, R. (2008) Dyslexia and Self-Concept: A Review of Past Research with Implications for Future Action, in G. Reid, A. Fawcett, F. Manis and L. Siegel (eds), *The SAGE Handbook of Dyslexia*, London, SAGE

Flora, S. (2000) Praise's Magic Reinforcement Ratio: Five to One Gets the Job Done, *The Behaviour Analyst Today*, 1, 4, 62–9

McNicholas, J. and McEntee, J. (1991, 2004) *Games to Improve Reading Levels*, NASEN/Routledge

Riddick, B. (2010) *Living with Dyslexia* (2nd edn), Abingdon, David Fulton/Routledge

Rochat, P. (2003) Five Levels of Self-awareness as they Unfold Early in Life, *Consciousness and Cognition*, 12, 4, 717–31

Rose, Sir J. (2009) *Identifying and Teaching Children and Young People with Dyslexia and Literacy Difficulties*, Nottingham, DCSF

Scott, R. (2004) *Dyslexia and Counselling*, London, Whurr

Verschueren, K., Doumen, S. and Buyse, E. (2012) Relationships with Mother, Teacher, and Peers: Unique and Joint Effects on Young Children's Self-concept, *Attachment and Human Development*, 14, 3, 233–48

Zafeirakou, A. (2012) *The Quest for Access, Quality and Equity in Early Childhood Education (ECE)*, PowerPoint presentation at the Athens Global Partnership For Education/UNICEF regional workshop, available online at: http://www.unicef.org

Zentall, S. and Morris, B. (2012) A Critical Eye: Praise Directed Toward Traits Increases Children's Eye Fixations on Errors and Decreases Motivation, *Psychonomic Bulletin and Review*, 19, 6, 1073–7

Chapter 5

Wider learning characteristics associated with dyslexia

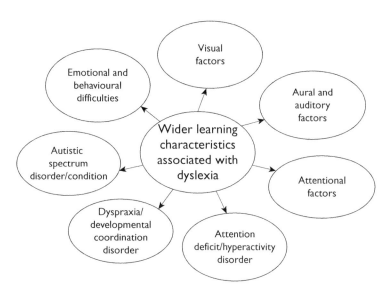

Good practice points

For good practice we need to:

1. adopt dyslexia-aware practice from earliest stages;
2. appreciate that differences in learning characteristics may overlap with dyslexia;
3. be alert to the emotional and behavioural impact of dyslexia when literacy is developing, ensuring that teasing or bullying do not take place;
4. tune our own verbal performance to make it as audible as possible, without shouting;
5. quiet our classrooms when literacy and numeracy are required.

Overlapping learning characteristics

There has been growing recognition that for many children who experience dyslexia or possible dyslexia, there may be other learning characteristics involved. There are varying views about co-occurrence; some feel that dyslexia is rarely a learning characteristic that exists by itself, others believe that specific learning difficulties are themselves related to each other. Since human characteristics, including learning characteristics, exist within a range of distribution, it is not surprising if some dyslexic learners have other learning characteristics of greater or lesser prominence. Deponio (2004) identifies dyspraxia, attention deficit/hyperactivity disorder and specific language impairment as of particular relevance in a discussion of dyslexia; dyslexia may also co-occur with mathematics difficulty (specific language impairment is discussed in Chapter 7 and mathematics in Chapter 9).

Visual factors

An important strand in the discussion of dyslexia, its nature and the ways in which it can be helped has focused on visual factors. In searching for a causal theory, considerable research has gone into exploring how eyes react and how visual messages are interpreted in the brain when reading is taking place. Included within this area of exploration is research concerning coloured overlays and lenses.

Visual factors are concerned with how eyes respond in the reading process, and how print is recognised within a reader's brain. Eyes fix on different points within a word in the reading process and they make rapid eye movements known as saccades; this is an unconscious process. Considerable research effort has gone into exploring whether there are anomalous characteristics in the way dyslexic children focus upon words in order to read them. The role of the magnocellular pathway forms part of this research, examining the way in which visual input about motion and depth perception is processed and interpreted by a brain (Stein, 2001).

Research concerning the stability of the visual image of letters and words when dyslexia readers are tackling them has been considerable. An interrogation of visual (binocular) instability has contributed to a research focus on visual stress, or 'visual disruption'. This term is now commonly used to describe the effect of words moving about, or subject to other distortions for readers, and has a relationship with research into the impact of coloured overlays and lenses (Wilkins, 1996). As with other aspects of dyslexia research, the visual account of dyslexia is contested and research continues.

From the point of view of practice, if the effect is only that of increasing confidence, then coloured overlays or lenses can still provide valuable support. Assessment by a behavioural optometrist and the prescription of coloured lenses may take place, once a regular eye test has ruled out any other visual problems. More usually, assessment within school may occur, particularly if a child says that when they try to read, the print does not remain stable. Where coloured overlays are in use, it is important to know that a colour preference can change with time.

It is thought that about 50 per cent of people who experience dyslexia will experience visual stress. However, visual stress or disruption is not necessarily associated with dyslexia;

it can be experienced by people who are not dyslexic. Scotopic sensitivity syndrome, or Meares-Irlen syndrome, are terms used to describe the experience of visual disruption of this kind, although the validity of the construct continues to be debated. Some professionals believe that the impact of coloured lenses or overlays is only that of a placebo – that there is no real effect. Nevertheless, first-person accounts indicate that sometimes coloured overlays can help.

Aural and auditory factors

Aural input and processing also have been scrutinised for possible causal explanations of dyslexia. One of the characteristics of dyslexia is a difficulty in identifying speech sounds, especially in relation to their visual, written expression. Hearing checks will not identify this, and may lead to frustration as parents and carers, practitioners and learners themselves seek to clarify an apparent hearing difficulty when there is no biological hearing problem evident.

However, there are also some physiological aspects that affect auditory processing. Lindsay Peer's (2009) work on glue ear (Otitis Medea) identifies a much higher than expected proportion of people with dyslexia who have experienced this difficulty. Peer considers that glue ear, compromising auditory input, prevents normal auditory processing development from taking place and that its impact continues well into adulthood, after the condition itself has disappeared. She considers that glue ear not only affects correct hearing of phonological input, but that the effect of glue ear extends to balance (through the role of the inner ear in sensing and maintaining human balance), eye movement, short-term memory and speed of processing. Peer's research indicates that dyslexic learners who have, or have had, glue ear, experience dyslexia more severely. In addition, a dyslexic learner experiencing glue ear must also contend with pain. Peer also considers that there is a detrimental emotional impact to the effect of glue ear, resulting from the frustration and uncertainty of not being able to hear speech correctly.

Ziegler and his co-authors identify a further external impact upon auditory perception in the form of noise. They found that children's dyslexic difficulties were exacerbated by noisy classrooms and cited Jamieson et al.'s (2004) research, stating that '[t]he average noise in a primary school classroom is about 72 dB(A), which is enough to reduce speech intelligibility by over 50%' (Ziegler et al., 2009: 742). The purpose of Ziegler et al.'s research was to explore more deeply how the auditory perception of children with dyslexia was affected by noise, compared to that of children with a specific language impairment. Generally, listeners make use of the small gaps between noise levels to deduce what is being said, but the researchers concluded that it takes many clues for an intending reader to overcome the impact of noise and that this was particularly difficult for children who experienced dyslexia.

Current auditory research focuses upon neurological aspects of how dyslexic people hear and respond to speech sounds. Goswami's recent research is concerned with the frequency of sound signals, and how they are interpreted by dyslexic learners. Her temporal sampling theory indicates that it is difficult for people who experience dyslexia to hear the rhythmic stresses of syllables, and to carry over a sense of the rhythms and patterns in a word (Goswami, 2011). This has an impact upon phonological perception.

The temporal sampling theory states that dyslexic learners have cognitive difficulty in synchronising auditory systems; synchronisation is of considerable interest in current dyslexia research. Breznitz's (2008) whole-brain theory considers that dyslexia occurs when there is a mismatch of timing between aural information and visual information within neurological processing. Other efforts are in hand to reconcile the different theoretical perspectives on dyslexia (Goswami *et al.*, 2014).

Attentional factors

It is understandable if we think of attentional issues as being concerned with pupils' focus upon a practitioner. Pupils may appear distracted or disengaged, and to some practitioners this is an expression of disobedience or lack of readiness to learn. However, attention has an internal and an external aspect. When teachers request attention they are seeking external evidence of voluntary concentration; but attention can also be an unconscious, cognitive process.

The events and items that attract our attention are governed by a number of factors. While we can make a conscious effort to notice things, generally attention is an unconscious process until we direct it. Michael Posner and his colleagues examine the nature of attention for both its neurological basis and its implications for education (see, for example, Posner and Rothbart, 2014). Posner considers that there are three attentional networks to consider: the alerting, orienting and executive networks. The alerting network operates in a young infant, who notices events that attract his or her sensory attention; the orienting network operates when a child's attention is drawn to items or events that are being carried out nearby. Posner considers that the executive network, which is concerned with resolving competing claims on attention and with directing attention voluntarily, only starts to operate at around four years old.

The implications of this for early learning are considerable: they suggest that a very young child may be stimulated by sensory input and that a child who is a little older may have their attention attracted by adults who want them to focus in a particular direction. However, asking young children to pay attention is not going to have much impact until they have learnt to direct their attention voluntarily; this involves some maturation in a child's brain. Voluntary attention involves self-regulation, calling on the executive attention network, and is an important skill in children's educational development.

Attention deficit/hyperactivity disorder

Attention and self-regulation are sometimes so difficult for children as to be disabling. The characteristic of attention deficit disorder (ADD)/attention deficit hyperactivity disorder (ADHD), like many other aspects of special educational needs, is controversial. In some ways it has taken the place of the obsolete term 'maladjusted', with pupils sometimes described as experiencing ADHD when they will not respond to engagement or control. The term 'attention deficit disorder' has been used in describing a child who does not have the hyperactivity aspects to their behaviour, but who may be distracted and unfocused, a state commonly described as 'daydreaming'. *DSM-5* includes the diagnostic category of AD/HD, the separation of AD and HD suggesting 'either/or' hyperactivity. ICD-10 also includes attention deficit disorder with and without hyperactivity.

The term 'ADHD', as it is more commonly used, is more likely to describe a child who is restless and has difficulty keeping their attention on one thing; ADHD has been described as paying attention to too many things, rather than not paying attention at all. This places a different perspective on the term and suggests that practitioners need to do more to help a child focus their attention. Restlessness and fidgeting will not be controlled for long by a teacher's instruction or discipline; some practitioners will give small objects to a child to enable them to discharge their fidgety tendency. Doodling, a practice carried out by many, can be another such displacement activity.

As practitioners, we may need to do more for a child whose attention is not captured, internally or externally, by the requirements of literacy tasks. It will not help to castigate a child for not paying attention. Instead, we need to make use of our professional skills to deliver learning in small, interesting chunks that make use of multisensory methods and give children something active to do. Some practitioners advocate placing a child with ADHD near the front of a class so that there is less opportunity for distraction from surroundings. A pupil can then focus on a practitioner, and a practitioner can see when a pupil has lost that focus and return them to their task.

Dyspraxia/developmental coordination disorder

Developmental coordination disorder, more commonly known as dyspraxia, is a motor coordination difficulty, affecting both gross and fine motor skills, and like all specific learning difficulties it is manifested within a range. In the past, children with this kind of difficulty in a mild form would have been thought of as 'clumsy'. Deponio (2004) notes that the relationship of dyslexia and dyspraxia have been of interest to researchers for some time. She gives the incidence for overlap as falling in the region of 50 per cent, drawing on the literature to indicate that 50 per cent of dyslexic children experience characteristics associated with dyspraxia, and 40–5 per cent of dyspraxic children experience dyslexia (citing Kaplan 1998 and Portwood, 1999).

As with other specific learning difficulties there is an internal, cognitive aspect to dyspraxia as well as the external characteristic of motor difficulty. Kirby *et al.* (2010) consider that a dyspraxic child's motor difficulties are the result of reduced cognitive planning or execution of movement. They are not the result of physiological difficulties, but of the cognitive process known as executive function. This has impact upon movement so that daily tasks, manipulative skills and physical endeavours are all affected. In addition, Kirby *et al.* consider that difficulties with the planning and carrying out of movement extend to affecting how a child copes with having tasks directed, with managing several tasks at once, with carrying out tasks in order, with tasks that require thinking through and with the organising of elements in a sequence.

Just as potential dyslexia might look like literacy immaturity in a young child, dyspraxia might look like immaturity of movement. However, there is also the cognitive aspect to consider. The Dyspraxia Foundation states that not only will a dyspraxic preschool child have motor coordination difficulties and delays, he or she may also need specific teaching of skills; instinctive or intuitive learning cannot be assumed (Dyspraxia Foundation, 2014). A child may also experience verbal dyspraxia, affecting articulation of speech. One dyslexia theory links movement and automaticity with phonology and speed of processing, through the involvement of the cerebellum (Fawcett and Nicolson 2004). As in dyslexia, a practitioner will want to observe whether a child's difficulty in carrying out motor tasks and associated executive planning seems unusual and longstanding.

Autistic spectrum disorder/condition

Until recently, diagnoses distinguished between Asperger's syndrome and autistic spectrum disorder or condition (ASC or ASD). However, Asperger's syndrome is no longer recognised in *DSM-5*. Instead, autism spectrum disorder is identified as having common characteristics over a range of difficulty, reflecting a modern perspective on learning difficulties. Autistic spectrum disorder or condition has for some time been associated with the triad of impairment, which states that people who experience this have difficulties in the areas of imagination, communication and social integration. *DSM-5* reduces this analysis to two domains, those of 'social communication' and 'restrictive, repetitive behaviours', categorised at three levels of need for support. It also introduces a new diagnosis of 'social communication disorder' (National Autistic Society, 2013).

Like other learning characteristics, autistic spectrum condition is expressed across a range. A child with severe autism is likely to have been identified at an early age, by health or multi-agency teams, while for some children, an identified diagnosis of autistic spectrum condition will not be made until later; for others there may be no formal diagnosis unless an impact upon daily living creates a need for further enquiry. A child who is attending a mainstream nursery, preschool or early years facility may experience identified or unidentified autism; practitioners are likely to be aware of communication needs, a restricted range of interests and play, isolated, individual activity and reluctance to be directed.

Most research about dyslexia and autism has been concerned with investigating whether there is a neurological relationship between the two (see, for example, Williams and Casanova, 2009). However, if literacy difficulties exist independently of other learning characteristics – a point which itself is debated – then it is to be expected that some children with ASC would experience dyslexia. Certainly, it is the case that some children with ASC find literacy learning to be arduous, but practitioners may feel that this is a result of a child's reluctance to respond to adult direction.

Rigidity of interpretation, lack of recognition of social context, dislike of particular words or word formats and preferences as to how, when and with whom reading takes place may all interfere with literacy acquisition for a child with ASC. Kate Nation and her co-authors (Nation *et al.*, 2006) found that literacy difficulty for children with ASC tends to fall in the area of comprehension, being linked to compromised understanding of language in context. The authors identified children with ASC who were not able to read, generally among the lower end of their age range of their sample (six to 15 years), but since this was not the focus of their research the literacy needs of these particular children were not investigated further.

Nevertheless, it would certainly seem possible to have a reading disorder co-occurring with autistic spectrum disorder; the UK National Autistic Society confirms this, referring to autism as co-occurring with other learning difficulties, including dyslexia. It might also be difficult to identify dyslexia as a characteristic existing independently from ASC; reading delay might be judged as resulting from the impact of ASC. It seems likely, then, that there are children whose dyslexia is masked by ASC; dyslexia should not be ruled out in these circumstances.

A child with ASC might be able to respond effectively to systematic phonics, delivered consistently to reinforce rules. Literacy tasks can be linked to a child's preferred activities, and the activities enjoyed by a child with ASC can be made into group activities in order to reinforce social communication. Jordan and Jones (1999) point out that a child with ASC has a full range of emotional responses; this could include the doubts and anxieties that can characterise experience of dyslexia. A practitioner can reduce anxiety by providing a learning environment that does not over-stimulate an already-anxious child with ASC. Providing a child with a quiet, calming area, such as a plain corner or carrel may help; although this is not what we expect from an early learning environment, it may be important in reducing stress for a young learner with ASC.

Emotional and behavioural difficulties

In the early years period, different learning characteristics start to become more visible. As Hartas (2006) has pointed out, the noticeable characteristics may be those of negative behaviour. A child who experiences autistic spectrum disorder or condition may make unusual responses to social interactions. A child who experiences difficulties with motor skills will attract the attention of practitioners when participating in gross or fine physical activities; there may also be expressions of frustration or reluctance to comply. Children who have difficulty with speech and language may adopt behavioural ways of communicating, not always acceptably. Other children may present aggressive, disruptive, or withdrawn behaviours that cause practitioners concern. When behaviours like these are prominent they take priority, whereas the possibility of dyslexia at this stage is present mostly as a potential, becoming noticeable only as peers' literacy skills advance.

Sadly, many dyslexic learners experience bullying; some sources believe that as many as 85 per cent of dyslexic children experience teasing, verbal abuse or physical abuse, perhaps several times a week (Riddick, 2010; Scott, 2004). Rosemary Scott considers that this begins to affect dyslexic learners at around the time that literacy difficulties become more noticeable, perhaps between eight and ten years old. She notes the peer dynamics that give rise to bullying, pointing out that children who are sad and lacking in confidence are vulnerable to being targeted. Scott points out that some dyslexic children may also bully others in a retaliatory way. Bullying is a complex matter and not simply solved; there are social and psychological factors and dynamics involved. Scott herself has no easy answers for the difficult situation of bullying. However, she believes that a child who is bullied is abused on two levels: by the bully and by the adult who does nothing about it.

Practitioners will need to be alert to the risk of bullying starting to emerge as children gain, or fail to gain, literacy skills. Adults should discourage any such tendencies while children are young and, at the same time, make sure that they, themselves, do not make examples of dyslexic children, even in well-meaning ways. Riddick notes that dyslexic children are constantly afraid of teasing and work hard to disguise their dyslexia or to avoid it being noticed.

Dyslexia-aware principles: supporting wider aspects of learning associated with dyslexia

From a consideration of wider aspects associated with dyslexia, several principles emerge:

- It is important to know that a child with possible dyslexia may not be seeing, or hearing, as we expect, even though there are no problems identified by hearing or sight checks.
- If there appear to be difficulties, we need to find alternative ways of getting our messages home. If a child seems to have difficulty decoding print, it is always worth considering whether their access is improved by the use of a coloured overlay.
- Knowing that someone may not be hearing as we expect them to hear, we may attend to our own presentation in order to make it as audible as possible.
- A practitioner who wants to improve their own practice can record themselves speaking and play it back to see how they sound.
- Practitioners need their voices to carry across distance without shouting. New educators can practice by standing at one end of a hall and making sure that a friend placed at the other end can hear them clearly.
- To support children's possible information processing difficulties when we are using oral/aural input, we can assist children by:
  o speaking as clearly as possible;
  o not speaking too quickly;
  o not speaking for too long;
  o taking care not to run words together;
  o putting pauses between instructions or comments to allow time for a child to process information;
  o giving instructions in short sequences, supported by visual or written cues.

Dyslexia-aware practice: a dyslexia-aware approach for early childhood

What can a dyslexia-aware approach mean for preschool children and for infants who are even younger? It is recognised that dyslexia cannot be cured or 'disappeared', but it can be ameliorated and often overcome for most intents and purposes. Practitioners, parents and carers can adopt dyslexia-aware practices from the start of a young child's journey into language and literacy, aiding the processes of coping and building strategies for a child who may be developing dyslexia.

All children, but especially children who experience potential or actual dyslexia:

- need considerable support for their confidence when undertaking literacy tasks;
- need differentiation of tasks, focusing upon quality rather than quantity;
- need attention to materials and resources so that print is easy to read and understand;
- need multisensory input;
- need opportunities to give their output in multisensory ways;
- need access and permission to use a variety of means for expressing their knowledge and understanding;
- benefit from knowing where learning is going – seeing the big picture;
- need a supportive attitude, understanding, technique and empathy from older children and from surrounding adults.

Foundational activities that can be carried out both by practitioners and by caregivers include: drawing, reading, singing and story-telling, with adults or other children. Skills would likewise include clapping rhythms and singing rhymes, alphabet recognition and pronunciation of letter sounds. Dyslexic learners often report issues with the small, similar words, such as in, it, at, am, an, on, of, if, etc., so work to establish these, backing them up with little drawings, will be useful. Talking activities such as inviting a child to describe or narrate something, speaking in longer phrases and sentences and asking for them back can help to extend vocabulary and language use. An adult can say 'tell me a story', or 'tell me some more about ...' to encourage talk to continue; an adult can repeat the child's last phrase back to them; then, usually, the narrator will carry on.

Information and communication technology: the impact of internet and digital use

The impact of ICT upon learning and child development has been of considerable interest to researchers for some time. Research has explored many facets of children's response to electronic resources, covering a wide range of technology that includes game playing, internet use, electronic reading, training and tuition through electronic means, and use of text-to-speech. As Miller and Warschauer point out, 'With the advent of tablet devices, the entire context of e-reading has been transformed' (Miller and Warschauer, 2013: 288).

They point out the ease with which such devices are used and the proliferation of apps addressed to the learning and literacy needs of young children. In reviewing research, the authors found that while electronic devices such as e-readers, tablets and electronic dictionaries helped children to engage with literacy learning, they did not replace text-based resources. Although electronic resources allow children to change fonts and page colours, and support learning through use of animation or text-to-speech, their place is seen as an integral part of teaching and learning, rather than as a substitute for traditional media. As vehicles for a game-based approach, they have the capacity to engage children's interest vividly, but as educational tools they are most likely to be effective when supported by adult involvement.

With technological change on this scale, concerns have arisen as to whether electronic interactions are, of themselves, changing young brains. All learning 'changes brains' since it is the nature of learning to forge new cognitive connections, but there are concerns that electronic interactions do this in a way that has not been seen before. Howard-Jones explores these issues for the Nominet Trust, an organisation that funds and supports the innovative use of internet technology, and which is maintained by a major internet registry. In a detailed consideration of the issues, he concludes that the most significant risks are found in the social contexts of use rather than in neurological impact. These consist of risks to wellbeing from:

- [a]n increase in aggressive response from playing violent video games;
- excessive use of computers/internet access/gaming that interferes with psychosocial wellbeing;
- attentional and vision problems;
- evening use of technology that leads to disrupted sleep (and related consequences).

(Howard-Jones, 2011: 64)

The author calls on parents to guide and regulate the use of electronic and digital resources, but this may be difficult, given the attractions of social media and digital devices. Getting children used to such controls from an early age would seem to be indicated.

Older children and parents tend to report play use of about two hours a day, above any school use. However, children who experience potential or actual dyslexia are likely to be already fatigued after literacy tasks, and fatigue makes dyslexia more apparent. Wellbeing is not only a matter of restricting the hours spent in electronic play; a gap between play and sleep would be advisable also to allow for thinking and excitement to 'wind down'.

Learning game: All Change – Developing body image and knowledge about names of parts of the body

Children go into pairs. A practitioner calls out 'Shoulder to shoulder', and children stand shoulder to shoulder; toe to toe etc. On the call 'All change' children find new partners.

Adapted from McNicholas and McEntee (1991, 2004), no. 1: Develop Body Image – All Change (p. 6).

How can dyslexia be supported in this game?

- A practitioner can wait until everybody has arrived in the right place before giving the next instruction.
- If a child does not find a partner or is left out, the next round could be structured as groups of threes. This would demand more organisation but could also create laughter, and would allow a potentially dyslexic child to take cues from his or her peers.
- A child for whom a practitioner wanted to develop language or body knowledge could be made the 'caller'. Turns could also be taken for this.

Attitude, knowledge, technique, empathy: supporting overlapping learning difficulties

Although it may seem a complicated matter to attend to a range of learning difficulties, there are some key concepts:

- *attitude*: remaining buoyant when faced with complex learning situations, taking hold of them by prioritising, creating interventions, monitoring, evaluating and seeking advice;
- *knowledge*: knowing how learning difficulties might overlap;
- *technique*: using clear, unambiguous, multisensory teaching addressed directly to individuals as well as to a whole class or group;
- *empathy*: being aware of underlying distress and of the potential for bullying.

Recommended reading

1. Bowen, M. and Plimley, L. (2008) *The Autism Inclusion Toolkit*, London, SAGE
2. Peterson, R. and Pennington, B. (2012) Seminar: Developmental Dyslexia, *Lancet*, 379 9830, 1997–2007, available online at: http://europepmc.org/

3. Howard-Jones, P. (2011) *The Impact of Digital technologies on Human Wellbeing*, Oxford, Nominet Trust, available online at: http://www.nominettrust.org.uk/knowledgecentre/. The article can be searched for under the author's name.

Useful websites

1. http://www.educationscotland.gov.uk/
   This website has an early years section in the left-hand menu. Deirdre Grogan's useful videos on the topic of holding pupils' attention can be found by accessing the items or using the search window.
2. http://www.dyspraxiafoundation.org.uk/
   The Dyspraxia Foundation website offers comprehensive advice. For information about dyspraxia at preschool age and dyspraxia's impact upon literacy, access the About Dyspraxia page and choose from items in the right-hand menu.
3. http://www.hi2u.org.uk
   This website is written by and for people who experience dyslexia, attention deficit/hyperactivity disorder, dyspraxia, Asperger's syndrome (autism) and other hidden difficulties. It contains first-person accounts and experiential tips and items that the website's author (Andy Hayes) and others have found useful.

MY DYSLEXIA EXPERIENCE: LISTENING TO CHILDREN

Children have told me that they have been shouted at by adults for not listening and not following instructions when in fact they had not heard, could not remember or felt that everything had been spoken too quickly for them to follow. I was told that, at times, they had missed out on social activities as they had not heard them or had not grasped the rules of games in the playground. (Peer, 2009: 39)

References

Bowen, M. and Plimley, L. (2008) *The Autism Inclusion Toolkit*, London, SAGE

Breznitz, Z. (2008) The Origin of Dyslexia: The Asynchrony Phenomenon, in G. Reid, A. Fawcett, F. Manis and L. Siegel (eds), *The SAGE Handbook of Dyslexia*, London, SAGE

Deponio, P. (2004) The Co-occurrence of Specific Learning Difficulties: Implications for Identification and Assessment, in G. Reid and A. Fawcett (eds), *Dyslexia in Context: Research, Policy and Practice*, London, Whurr

Dyspraxia Foundation (2014) *About Dyspraxia*, available online at: http://www.dyspraxiafoundation.org.uk/

Fawcett, A. and Nicolson, R. (2004) Dyslexia: the role of the cerebellum, in G. Reid and A. Fawcett (eds), *Dyslexia in Context: Research Policy and Practice*, London, Whurr.

Goswami, U. (2011) A Temporal Sampling Framework for Developmental Dyslexia, *Trends in Cognitive Sciences*, 15, 1, 3–10

Goswami, U., Power, A., Lallier, M. and Facoetti, A. (2014) Oscillatory 'Temporal Sampling' and Developmental Dyslexia: Toward an Over-arching Theoretical Framework, *Frontiers in Human Neuroscience*, 8, article 9, 1–3

Hartas, D. (2006) *Dyslexia in the Early Years*, Abingdon, Routledge

Howard-Jones, P. (2011) *The Impact of Digital Technologies Upon Human Wellbeing*, Oxford, Nominet Trust, available online at: http://www.nominettrust.org.uk/

Jamieson, D., Kranjc, G., Yu, K. and Hodgetts, W. (2004) Speech Intelligibility of Young School-Aged Children in the Presence of Real-Life Classroom Noise, *Journal of the American Academy of Audiology*, 15, 7, 508–17

Jordan, R. and Jones, G. (1999) *Meeting the Needs of Children with Autistic Spectrum Disorders*, London, David Fulton

Kaplan, B. (1998) Developmental Coordination Disorder – How Do You Define What It Is and What It Is Not?, paper presented at the Novartis Foundation Meeting, October

Kirby, A., Sugden, D. and Edwards, L. (2010) Developmental Co-ordination Disorder (DCD): More than Just a Movement Difficulty, *Journal of Research in Special Educational Needs*, 10, 3, 206–15

McNicholas, J. and McEntee, J. (1991, 2004) *Games to Improve Reading Levels*, NASEN/Routledge

Miller, E. and Warschauer, M. (2013) Young Children and e-reading: Research to Date and Questions for the Future, *Learning, Media and Technology*, 39, 3, 283–305

Nation, K., Clarke, P., Wright, B. and Williams, C. (2006) Patterns of Reading Ability in Children with Autism Spectrum Disorder, *Journal of Autism and Developmental Disorders*, 36: 911–19

National Autistic Society (2013) *Proposed Changes to Autism and Asperger Syndrome Diagnostic Criteria*, London, National Autistic Society, available online at: http://www.autism.org.uk

Peer, L. (2009) Dyslexia and Glue Ear: A Sticky Educational Problem, in G. Reid (ed.), *The Routledge Companion to Dyslexia*, Abingdon, Routledge

Peterson, R. and Pennington, B. (2012) Seminar: Developmental Dyslexia, *Lancet*, 379 9830, 1997–2007, available online at: http://europepmc.org/

Portwood, M. (1999) *Developmental Dyspraxia: Identification and Intervention*, London, David Fulton

Posner, M. and Rothbart, M. (2014) Attention to Learning of School Subjects, *Trends in Neuroscience and Education*, 2, 14–17

Riddick, B. (2010) *Living with Dyslexia* (2nd edn), Abingdon, David Fulton/Routledge

Scott, R. (2004) *Dyslexia and Counselling*, London, Whurr

Stein, J. (2001) The Magnocellular Theory of Developmental Dyslexia, *Dyslexia*, 7, 12–36

Wilkins, A. (1996) Helping Reading with Colour, *Dyslexia Review*, 7, 3, 4–7

Williams, E. and Casanova, M. (2009) Autism and Dyslexia: A Spectrum of Cognitive Styles as Defined by Minicolumnar Morphometry, *Medical Hypotheses*, 74, 59–62

Ziegler, J., Pech-Georgel, C., George, F. and Lorenzi, C. (2009) Speech-perception-in-noise Deficits in Dyslexia, *Developmental Science*, 12, 5, 732–45

Chapter 6

Dyslexia in the context of English as an alternative language

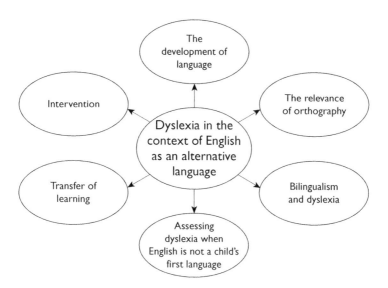

Good practice points

For good practice we need to:

1. consider, but not assume, dyslexia if a child is struggling with literacy in learning English language;
2. recognise the value of first language alongside the English-language learning that we seek to develop;
3. involve parents and caregivers in our joint efforts to support the development of literacy, knowing that development in a home language will also support developments in a new one;
4. teach phonological knowledge, but teach also words and morphemes, as these may be easier for a dyslexic learner to hear and to master;
5. teach alphabetic knowledge, as research shows this to be important for literacy development.

The relevance of orthography

Languages change and develop and, just as some English usage has changed, so too the role of English language in the world has changed. English is becoming a global language for business, entertainment and social communication, so that there is now a significant educational focus upon English as an alternative language (EAL). Social mobility and social change mean that many modern classrooms include children whose most familiar forms of speech are expressed in a range of different languages.

Education services may include specialists who are responsible for advising practitioners and for supporting children for whom English is not the first language. However, public services are always in great demand, so members of local communities may also be asked to advise and support. Some children whose English language skills may not yet be secure will also experience dyslexia. However, complicating factors associated with learning a new language make it hard for a practitioner to have a clear view about whether a young child's literacy is affected by a specific learning difficulty. While practitioners may still work in single-language settings, nevertheless, it is probably helpful for them to anticipate that young children with different languages may be attending their group or class in due course.

English is considered to be a difficult language because of its complexity; it is generally held that in English about 80 per cent of words are regular and can be decoded according to rules, while 20 per cent are not regular and have to be learnt individually. Ziegler and Goswami (2005) confirm that, in learning to speak and to read English, learners have to master language components at the letter level, the syllable level and the whole-word level. Letters can give more than one sound: 44 sounds are commonly reported; some sources suggest more – Habib (n.d.) suggests 48 in American English. Mastery of English language and literacy includes knowledge and correct use of vocabulary, morphology (understanding the form and structure of words), syntax and grammar, construction and discourse. Any and all of these can have pitfalls for a young learner who experiences potential or actual dyslexia.

English is the most complex of the Roman alphabet languages and is referred to as having a 'deep' orthography as opposed to a 'shallow' orthography. Shallow orthographies are phonologically regular: they have a close, systematic relationship between sounds as they are spoken and as they are written. Because of this deep orthography it takes longer for a child to gain functional literacy skills when their first language is English, than it does for a child whose first language has a more transparent, shallow orthography. Particular learning difficulties in reading, writing and spelling of English may be more obvious, or last for longer than would be expected.

Research into developmental dyslexia in other cultures, languages and orthographies has developed rapidly. Recent research shows that phonological characteristics may play a part even where orthographies are not based on the alphabetic system, although phonological aspects may not have the same dominance in those settings. Even when literacy does not involve mastering difficult phonological concepts, there can still be significant literacy difficulty among learners, generally characterised by a reduced speed of processing in literacy tasks. In addition, there may be specific difficulties associated with particular orthographies. Dyslexia can therefore be manifested differently in different languages, but, however it is expressed, the degree of difficulty in gaining necessary literacy skills may be commensurate with an identification of dyslexia.

Bilingualism and dyslexia

There are different kinds of bilingualism, just as there are different ways in which languages are used in modern society. Some children will have strong input from two languages from birth; others will be used to a single language in infancy and then they will learn one or more further languages later. Bilingual education contains its own issues, and Ferguson (2006) points out that there are ideological implications governing discussions of language education policy in this context. He describes tensions between a style of education that promotes the induction of all learners into, and through, the English language and another that promotes the maintenance of different languages; this is known as the assimilationist–pluralist debate.

Ferguson considers that the weight of evidence supports a form of bilingual education which educates a child in their first language as well as the second. Such practice is based on an understanding that developments in one language will support developments in the other. This is known as the additive model; Mortimore and her co-authors agree that it is important that a first language should continue to develop in this way (Mortimore *et al.*, 2012). They point out that the contrasting subtractive model, which does not address education in a child's first language, instead concentrating on assimilation into the classroom language, can undermine both languages and create a barrier to learning.

Mortimore and her co-authors discuss the range of contextual variables that may affect children's literacy when English is a new language for them. Noting the lack of research into cultural aspects that may affect the task of learning English as a new language, they point out a range of complicating factors: cultural, orthographic, educational, motivational, family- and data-based. There are emotional, experiential and economic aspects to new language learning; there may be different expectations of teaching and learning in process, practice and usage, and different characteristics in the language structure itself, affecting a pupil's expectations. There may be misunderstandings and assumptions based on low attainment in the new language and other assumptions about children's wish to learn the new language. Finally, data and record-keeping may not reflect the complexity of context. Factors such as these can make it extremely difficult for a practitioner to know the cause of barriers in a young child's new language learning.

Transfer of learning

The issue of transfer of learning is important in the context of language teaching because of the effect of one language upon another, and the understanding that progress in one language aids progress in the other. The mechanisms governing transfer of learning are not yet fully known, but they also have relevance to the context of dyslexia, owing to the need for children to transfer new learning in literacy into other contexts. One of the main goals of literacy teaching of young children is that they should be able to generalise sounds or spellings so that they can be read or spelt correctly, in a process that becomes automatic. However, it is characteristic of dyslexia is that this does not happen easily.

While acknowledging the range of theories about transfer to learning, Goldstone and Day (2012) identify three recent themes. These include: first, the point of view and attitude to learning of a learner; and, second, their motivation, bearing in mind that transfer of learning requires cognitive work and a learner has to be willing to undertake this. These two themes signal the importance of affective aspects of teaching and learning. As a third theme, Goldstone and Day point to a need to teach learners with a range of methods that establish flexibility in thinking. This raises questions as to how far literacy teaching and learning address generalisation of learning, whether more could be done and also how far dyslexia has a constraining effect upon this transfer.

Considering the role of marking and correcting work in encouraging transfer of learning, Butler *et al.* (2013) conclude that explaining a correct answer in important. Feedback that includes explanation is more likely to provide understanding that will transfer to further learning than simply marking work right or wrong, or correcting it without explanation. This suggests a style of teaching and learning that requires practitioners to give explanations of why a certain practice is the right or best way to do something. This includes the require-ment of making sure that a child has understood.

Assessing dyslexia when English is not a child's first language

A dyslexia-aware practitioner is likely to notice children who are not making sufficient lit-eracy progress over time, whose rate of progress is slow and who may be avoiding, or becoming distressed over, literacy tasks. He or she also needs this vigilance when working with a child for whom English is not the first language. A practitioner may notice memory, sequencing or organising difficulties and may contrast these with a student's strengths in areas that do not depend on literacy.

Where a teacher has access to a specialist support teacher, the specialist will be able to discuss whether a child is experiencing an unexpected level of difficulty with gaining literacy in their home language. This would be a useful indicator of an underlying difficulty. Once alerted, it is possible to carry out informal assessments such as those discussed in Chapter 3. It is also possible to notice whether resistant or avoidant behaviour coincides with literacy lessons and tasks, or whether a learner relies on the support of friends or a helper in literacy work.

The possibility of a more structured, psychometric assessment becomes problematic; tests may make use of nuance or idiom, and they may not be available in a child's first language. Norms are often based on expectations of performance by native English-language speakers at a certain age, but for children whose first language is not English, age-based norms may not be comparable. For learners acquiring English skills subsequent to their initial language, it is likely to take a number of years to reach the level of phonological fluency expected by tests and assessment instruments, when these have been based upon children who learnt English from infancy (Frederickson *et al.*, 1997; Kelly and Phillips, 2011).

Some assessment instruments, such as the *Phonogical Assessment Battery* (*PhAB*), have norms based on the expectations of children whose first language is not English (Frederickson *et al.*, 1997; Gibbs and Bodman, 2014). An assessment of this kind offers valuable diagnostic information, but, as Mortimore and her co-authors confirm in their research, it would be difficult to assess, or screen for, dyslexia in young learners whose first language is not English because of an array of possible complicating factors. Mortimore *et al.* warn that we should not rush to assign a child's struggle with English to the fact that it is an alternative language for them, but equally, we should not rush to assign the same difficulty to an identification of dyslexia. They suggest that when the language learning moves towards more academic characteristics it becomes clearer whether a child has a specific learning difficulty in literacy.

Even when there is no specific learning difficulty present, the process of alternative language acquisition may not proceed evenly in the ways that practitioners would expect for schoolwork. Cummins differentiates between 'basic interpersonal communicative skills (BICS)' and 'cognitive academic language proficiency (CALP)' for learners who are studying to acquire a new language (Cummins, 2008, citing his own earlier work in 1979–81). He makes the point that learners who are skilled at the BICS level give an impression of being fluent throughout the new language. In comparison, their academic work (CALP) may appear to be lagging, causing concern. Cummins believes that practitioners may not distinguish between these two aspects, leading to perceptions that children are experiencing learning difficulty. Such perceptions are compounded by assessment procedures that employ 'cognitive academic' language that a child has not yet learnt. A child who is fluent conversationally might, then, appear to have specific literacy difficulties in reading, spelling and written expression and find this borne out in assessment. A child with a profile like this might appear dyslexic but could catch up when CALP is in place.

Kelly and Phillips suggest some indicators for recognising dyslexia when children are learning English as a new language. These include: a noticeable difference between children's understanding of what is said to them and what they read; continuing difficulty with phonological awareness and skills when children have experienced a good level of teaching and have, themselves, an appropriate level of conversation; little engagement with written resources and books; little sign of automaticity developing in literacy (Kelly and Phillips, 2011: 89/90). In considering the English early years Foundation Stage profile, Snowling (2013) concludes that teachers' assessments of children are accurate and provide effective predictions for later literacy skills. In the case of very young children who are learning English as an alternative language, practitioners may need to have confidence in their own skilled judgements about literacy difficulty.

Intervention

While a general dyslexia-aware approach can do a great deal to help young learners master the difficulties of literacy in the English language, there is a risk that it could be seen as sufficient. Combined with modern, systematic approaches to phonics teaching, there may be a hope that changes of this sort will reduce issues of dyslexia. It must not be forgotten that dyslexia exists as a range and while some young people will manage to cope, there will be others who struggle throughout their schooling, and who exit with far lower levels of literacy than society expects.

There is agreement that, for young children who are struggling to learn English as an alternative language, additional programmes are likely to be required. This presents the issue of whether an intervention should focus on literacy or on language. Schneider (2009) points out that many cultures start teaching additional languages to young children within the early years range. Where language programmes are used, Schneider advises that these should be modified to reflect practices that support dyslexia, such as the careful arrangement of elements into short steps and sequences, exploitation of multisensory methods, individual tuition opportunities and opportunities to rehearse, revise and revisit the new learning.

Kelly and Phillips consider that children who are struggling to gain English language skills may need a structured, systematic literacy programme alongside the EAL input that they receive. Their own Conquering Literacy programme (Kelly and Phillips, 2011) is a modern, comprehensive programme of this kind. The programme is described as being for children between four and 16 years, and, like other highly structured programmes, it is designed specifically to help children to overcome dyslexia by teaching the elements of English language methodically and consistently.

Mortimore *et al.*'s (2012) research addressed the interface of dyslexia and the acquisition of English as an alternative language. Their sample was of primary school children who were older than the early years group. However, the research team's findings are of interest and relevance for practitioners who work with younger children. The children in the study had English as an additional language and were identified as disadvantaged in literacy to the extent that they might well be dyslexic. The authors created two programmes of intervention, comparing these with a control group. One programme was based on ICT and print-based resources, the other centred upon paired reading. Both programmes delivered gains in literacy, with some differences; the ICT programme specifically aided spelling and phonological decoding, whereas the paired reading supported a broader profile of literacy skills.

The research uncovered the complicating factors that might make it difficult to be certain about dyslexia in a child with EAL. Nevertheless, valuable gains were made and could reasonably be attributed to the combination of the factors and attributes in the programme. This confirms Gavin Reid's point that the pedagogy needed for dyslexic learners is not so much different in nature, as different in density, or intensity (Reid, 2005). This intense intervention, instigated by Mortimore *et al.* and implemented by well-trained and well-supported practitioners, made a considerable difference to the literacy of the pupils in the study. There is no reason why similar techniques should not be used with younger learners, but for greatest effect they would need to be supported by training and by recording, monitoring and evaluation.

Dyslexia-aware principles: a multisensory approach

Both multilingual challenges and literacy challenges can benefit from a dyslexia-aware approach, focusing upon multisensory work and the ways known of helping learners who experience dyslexia. Mortimore *et al.* confirm that a dyslexia-aware approach to literacy will help multilingual learners who are struggling with gaining English and literacy skills, and who might also experience dyslexia.

The term 'multisensory' sometimes has a specific meaning in dyslexia pedagogy; it is used to describe the longstanding Orton–Gillingham method, which consists of following a systematic, structured programme covering all the elements of English literacy. In this context, multi-sensory working refers to looking at the word, listening to it, reading it and writing it, all as simultaneously as possible. The focus remains upon traditional literacy technique and skills. Present-day approaches to multisensory learning use stimuli more widely – following a visual-auditory-kinaesthetic approach. Children may write a letter or word in sand, in water on the ground, in huge letters and in three-dimensional ones, creating pictures or diagrams, or modelling in clay. They may play physical games that have words as part of the game. Practitioners explore a wide range of tactile and sensory stimuli in order to help children retain literacy knowledge.

Multisensory techniques of this kind are normal practice in early years and preschool settings. However, for a dyslexic learner, especially when English is not his or her first language, multi-sensory literacy work may have to continue for a considerable time, perhaps into secondary school or beyond. In these instances, the deciding factor is concerned with what practices a learner will accept as helpful stimuli without embarrassment.

Dyslexia-aware practice: paired reading

Originally seen as a means of structuring parents' help for children practising reading at home, paired reading continues to be endorsed for use by parents and by education settings alike. Paired reading was recommended in the Brooks report *What Works for Children With Literacy Difficulties? The Effectiveness of Intervention Schemes* (Brooks, 2002). Its value is in developing word recognition, fluency and confidence, and with increased reading skill may come increases in other aspects of literacy. Comprehension could be aided by adding conversation about the text, but one of the characteristics of paired reading is that it is meant to be a comfortable, reassuring and supportive activity, so any conversation of this kind should be naturalistic rather than a questioning of the reader.

The pairing consists of a reader and a skilled helper. They read a text aloud simultaneously; with experience the helper can delay their own reading minimally so that the reader is taking the lead, without feeling under pressure to do so. When the reader feels confident, he or she gives a prearranged signal and continues to read alone. If he or she is defeated by a word, the helper can supply it, after a pause to allow their reader a chance to recall it. The pair then continues to read together until a reader feels confident to continue alone. The text has to be manageable for a reader.

In current practice, paired reading is sometimes amalgamated with peer tutoring, otherwise known as a 'buddy system' of reading practice. In a paired reading system of this kind, more highly skilled children, likely to be older, help younger ones to read. It has long been a tradition in primary schools that older children help younger ones in this way. However, paired reading needs training; a helper needs to know how to guide a young reader and to praise them appropriately. A demonstration video of peer-tutored paired reading is available on http://www.tes.co.uk/.

Paired reading is designed to increase the skill of reading in context, lending itself to a more confident approach to reading. However tempting, it would not be the place to undertake an analysis of sounds, or to introduce a memory intervention for a lost word. In order to maintain the ethos of paired reading, the best way to do this would perhaps be to make a note of problematic words and tackle them again later.

Information and communication technology: language learning

The use of audio-visual and communications media for the teaching of languages has a long pedigree and language learning for groups and individuals continues to develop through the use of ICT hardware and software. In addition to commercially available programs there are free language learning materials on internet websites and free language videos available on YouTube. Additionally, the development of language learning apps is a growth area.

A number of programs are available for use with young children and these vary in look, purpose, content, format and complexity – and in cost. Electronic or accented vocals are common, so, for this reason and for other reasons of support, it is advisable for a child to work with a familiar adult when accessing the programs. Research suggests that unfamiliar accents interfere initially with linguistic processing, although after a short time listeners will adapt. This is a mechanism that occurs across all the age ranges, but for the youngest children it may be particularly hard to recognise at first that an unfamiliar vocalisation equates to meaningful speech (Cristia *et al.*, 2012).

For young children with actual or potential dyslexia, one app which appears likely to be useful is Play and Learn LANGUAGES, designed for Android and 'i' operating systems. This is a free 'flashcard' app, based on sets of words linked to a topic, with a group of further packs of words available at a modest cost. Each word is spoken in a target language and in a home language and is accompanied by a clear, uncluttered picture, although a few of these are culture-specific and would be aided by an adult's support. Each pack is supported by a number of quiz or spelling games. Dyslexic learners are likely to benefit from the clarity of text and image, the simple effectiveness of the approach and the variety of activities available.

Play and Learn LANGUAGES is currently available in 19 languages, so can be used to support the learning of English as an alternative language for many children who are not native English-language speakers. A companion app is Bilingual Baby, which uses the same approach and similar images, but with fewer word-based games. Both of these apps focus upon vocabulary building.

Learning game: Tiddlywinks – a physical activity supporting word recognition

A card is drawn up with shapes for target areas and sounds/letters or simple words written in the shapes (see Figure 6.1). Each shape carries a score. Children play individually or in small groups. They flick counters onto the card in the traditional tiddlywinks manner and score if they read the sound/letters or words correctly. A3 card may be a better size than A4, although children might need to stretch to read it, because counters can travel over a distance when flicked.

A development of this game would be to number the shapes and refer children to a list that attaches letter/sounds or words to the numbers. An accompanying text that puts the words into context would add interest and support word recognition.

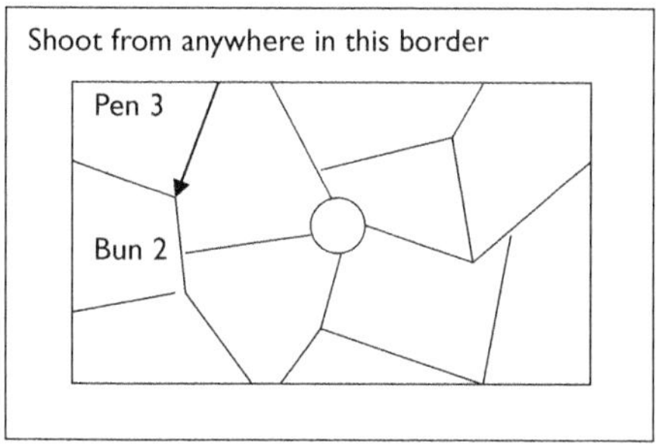

Figure 6.1 Tiddlywinks target area

Adapted from McNicholas and McEntee (1991, 2004), no. 35: Word Recognition – Tiddlywinks (p. 17).

How can dyslexia be supported in this game?

- Attaching literacy skills to a multisensory game ensures a greater chance of success for a potentially dyslexic child.
- To reduce over-competitiveness that may disadvantage potentially dyslexic learners, children can try to improve their own score rather than to beat someone else's score.
- If a separate wall/board list is provided of scores attached to targets, a dyslexia-aware practitioner will provide the list on the table, not only on a wall. This is because a dyslexic child may have difficulty with transferring the information, mentally, from one place to another.
- Prior preparation of the target letter/sounds or words will give a potentially dyslexic child a greater chance of success.

Attitude, knowledge, technique, empathy: being dyslexia-aware when working within a range of language experiences

Parents and caregivers want to help children with their literacy regardless of their own fluency in English, or the language used at home. Knowledge is increasing about the characteristics of dyslexia within a range of languages. We can support a wider experience of literacy development through:

- *attitude*: showing respect for different languages by making every effort to pronounce learners' home language correctly, such as in using names and a small, basic vocabulary of greetings and praise words;
- *understanding*: appreciating that a key guide to alerting practitioners to the possibility of dyslexia is a learner's literacy skill in their first language, and taking steps to find out the level at which this might be;
- *technique*: connecting new learning to older learning by, first, briefly reprising the older learning, establishing a learner's recall of this, and then showing how it links to the new.

For best effect, a phrase like 'Do you remember this?' can be supported with multisensory materials – pictures, models, actions;

- *empathy*: being aware of the great lack of confidence possible when a child not only struggles with new language concepts, but also experiences difficulty in gaining literacy skills. Asking ourselves what this would feel like can help us to assist children when they experience such double difficulty.

Recommended reading

1. Mortimore, T., Hansen, L., Hutchings, M., Northcote, A., Fernanado, J., Horobin, L., Saunders, K. and Everatt, J. (2012) *Dyslexia and Multilingualism: Identifying and Supporting Bilingual Learners who Might be at Risk of Developing SpLD/Dyslexia*, London, British Dyslexia Association
2. Schneider, E. (2009) Dyslexia and Foreign Language Learning, in G. Reid (ed.), *The Routledge Companion To Dyslexia*, Abingdon, Routledge
3. Cummins, J. (2008) BICS and CALP: Empirical and Theoretical Status of the Distinction, in B. Street and N. H. Hornberger (eds), *Encyclopedia of Language and Education, 2nd Edition, Volume 2: Literacy*, New York: Springer Science/Business Media LLC, pp. 71–83

Useful websites

1. http://www.bdadyslexia.org/about/projects/completed-projects
   This is the location for Mortimore *et al.* (2012). Dyslexia and Multilingualism.
2. http://www.playnlearn.mobi/
   This is the web address advertising Play and Learn LANGUAGES, created by SHIFT Interactive. The company is based in Sydney, Australia.
3. http://www.happychild.org.uk
   Project Happychild is a long-serving website which links children across the world through schools interchanges. It offers free educational resources, provided through the efforts of volunteer contributors. The website has 16 areas, covering a range of relevant topics; it holds thousands of multi-language worksheets and an English reading scheme. The website provides resources in 19 languages, including four different versions of Chinese.

MY DYSLEXIA EXPERIENCE: OUR BILINGUAL CHILDREN

Our two boys are bilingual; they speak one language with me and the other with their mum. They get on fine with that, they are both good speakers, you would say they were fluent. The older one, Jon, is reading fairly well in both languages, but his teachers have raised the question of dyslexia. He gets muddled with writing, he struggles with the structure, the grammar. Ben is only just beginning with the phonics, and he is getting a bit muddled with those too – it might be different if the languages were very separate, but they're not. We are looking for dual-language texts and bilingual software for when they get older. We don't want them to lose their ability to speak two languages. (Parent)

References

Brooks, G. (2002) *What Works for Children With Literacy Difficulties? The Effectiveness of Intervention Schemes*, Nottingham, DfES

Butler, A., Godbole, N. and Marsh, E. (2013) Explanation Feedback is Better Than Correct Answer Feedback for Promoting Transfer of Learning, *Journal of Educational Psychology*, 105, 2, 290–8

Cristia, A., Seidl, A., Vaughn, C., Schmale, R., Bradlow, A. and Floccia, C. (2012) Linguistic Processing of Accented Speech Across the Lifespan, *Frontiers in Psychology*, 3, 479, available online at: http://www.ncbi.nlm.nih.gov/pmc/articles/PMC3492798/

Cummins, J. (2008) BICS and CALP: Empirical and Theoretical Status of the Distinction, in B. Street and N. H. Hornberger (eds), *Encyclopedia of Language and Education, 2nd Edition, Volume 2: Literacy*, New York, Springer Science/Business Media LLC, pp. 71–83

Ferguson, G. (2006) *Language Planning and Education*, Edinburgh, Edinburgh University Press

Frederickson, N., Frith, U. and Reason, R. (1997) *Phonological Assessment Battery (PhAB)*, Swindon, GL Assessment

Gibbs, S. and Bodman, S. (2014) *Phonological Assessment Battery 2nd Edition Primary (PhAB 2 Primary)*, Swindon, GL Assessment

Goldstone, R. and Day, S. (2012) Introduction, New Conceptualizations of Transfer of Learning, *Educational Psychologist*, 47, 3, 149–52

Habib, A. (n.d.) *Language and its Components*, PowerPoint presentation, available online at: *uwf.edu/*

Kelly, K. and Phillips, S. (2011) *Teaching Literacy to Learners with Dyslexia*, London, SAGE

McNicholas, J. and McEntee, J. (1991, 2004) *Games to Improve Reading Levels*, NASEN/Routledge

Mortimore, T., Hansen, L., Hutchings, M., Northcote, A., Fernanado, J., Horobin, L., Saunders, K. and Everatt, J. (2012) *Dyslexia and Multilingualism: Identifying and Supporting Bilingual Learners who Might be at Risk of Developing SpLD/Dyslexia*, London, British Dyslexia Association, available online at: http://www.bdadyslexia.org.uk/about/projects/completed-projects

Reid, G. (2005) Dyslexia, in A. Lewis and B. Norwich (eds), *Special Teaching for Special Children?*, Maidenhead, Open University Press

Schneider, E. (2009) Dyslexia and Foreign Language Learning, in G. Reid (ed.), *The Routledge Companion To Dyslexia*, Abingdon, Routledge

Snowling, M. (2013) Early Identification and Interventions for Dyslexia: A Contemporary View, *Journal of Research in Special Educational Needs*, 13, 1, 7–14

Ziegler, J. and Goswami, U. (2005) Reading Acquisition, Developmental Dyslexia, and Skilled Reading Across Languages: A Psycholinguistic Grain Size Theory, *Psychological Bulletin*, 131, 1, 3–29

Chapter 7

Dyslexia and the emergence of reading, writing and spelling

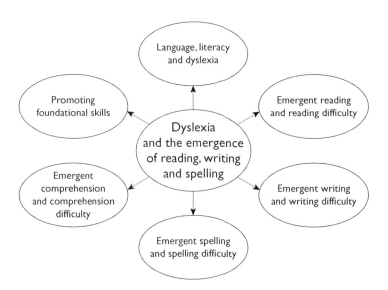

Good practice points

For good practice we need to:

1. support emergent literacy with a range of multisensory, foundational activities;
2. find ways to extend verbal language and vocabulary through focused talk;
3. provide a range of materials for mark-making, drawing and display;
4. provide a range of print experiences for young children, including books that use pictures only;
5. generate discussions about texts with the aim of developing comprehension.

Language, literacy and dyslexia

Babies are predisposed to gain language skills when they are presented with language as a stimulus. This begins with a sensory response and, soon after birth, babies can make a distinction between different speech sounds and also between the different patterns of rhythm and sound that are found within individual speech systems (prosody). Perani and her co-authors found that in the brains of very young infants this generates activity in both hemispheres (Perani *et al.*, 2011). As a child grows older, language centres in the brain become more specialised.

The earliest sounds made by babies are known as 'articulatory gestures', formed from a small number of consonants and vowels. This leads on to vocalisations which serve to create feedback, gaining responses from adults as to which sounds are perceived as approximating language and therefore carrying meaning. As a child grows older, maturing and developing, speech perception within his or her brain becomes more adult-like, although this takes several years to reach full development.

In the process of learning to talk, children's social environments extend, with imitation, education and natural curiosity helping children to develop both vocabulary and an understanding of the meaning of words. Similarly, grammar, syntax and comprehension develop both through education and through modifications experienced in daily life, within social and cultural contexts. Dooley points out that 'Young children's emergent comprehension experiences are likely to emerge from playful and/or caring experiences, and will be influenced by their social, cognitive and emotional qualities' (Dooley, 2011: 174).

The talk between children and adults can be aided when adults make sure that they talk in such a way as to open up dialogue, rather than to close it down. Children can be encouraged to say a little more and to move on from single-word answers; this is a matter of confidence as well as vocabulary. Talking in sentences, and expecting to get sentences spoken back, promotes an understanding of grammatical conventions at an early stage.

Talking is important for literacy in a number of ways. Children need to develop receptive and expressive language; the links between vocabulary and word decoding are important. If children do not recognise particular words as having meaning for them, they will find it harder to recognise them as meaningful in print. Children benefit from talking about the texts that they encounter; those texts can be about information and practical matters, as well as the usual stories of daily life or make-believe. Talking about texts at this stage can be conversational, rather than a questioning routine.

Dooley considers that the actual meanings that children assign to words and texts may be unexpected to adults, and may be specific to the children themselves. It is important that conversation about words and texts takes place, so that children may refine their understanding of vocabulary and their comprehension of text, and so that adults gain greater understanding of children's meaning-making.

As literacy develops, children who experience dyslexia are likely to keep to a smaller, restricted vocabulary that feels safe to write and spell. If practitioners do not make deliberate attempts to extend vocabulary and word usage it may transpire that dyslexic learners do not display the extent of their actual knowledge and understanding when writing. Two useful resources for promoting meaningful talking with young children are *Language for Learning* (Hayden and Jordan, 2007), and *Talking Time* (Dockrell and Stuart, 2007).

The question of how barriers to language-processing might arise, and the precise nature of such barriers, is the subject of ongoing research. One aspect of this concerns the question of whether or not a specific, cognitive, language impairment is directly related to dyslexia. Ramus and his co-authors explore this question, concluding that dyslexia and specific language impairment are two separate characteristics, but with considerable co-occurrence (Ramus *et al.*, 2013). While most children in their study experienced a phonological difficulty, some children with specific language impairment, and some children with dyslexia, did not. Between individuals and between groups, the phonological difficulties themselves were not always the same.

The authors are cautious in generalising about each group because of the amount of overlap between dyslexia and specific language difficulty. They describe children with specific language impairment (and without dyslexia) as being hampered in verbal expression, so that aspects of speech such as grammar, syntax, or tense are consistently underdeveloped, whereas children with dyslexia (but not specific language impairment) are hampered in reading but not in verbal expression. For practitioners working with very young children, distinctions of this kind will not be clear-cut and some children with apparent delays in their speech and language will improve with maturity. In both cases, it is the persistence and intractability of problems in the face of regular, effective teaching that alerts practitioners to the possible presence of a specific learning difficulty.

Emergent reading and reading difficulty

The term 'emergent literacy' is attributed to Marie Clay (Whitehurst and Lonigan, 1998). However, the authors point out that our understanding of how literacy emerges is complicated by different theorisations and understandings of literacy. The concept of emergent literacy embeds literacy learning within a social and developmental context. This view holds that there is no special point at which literacy begins; children's development encompasses skills, knowledge and attitudes that will be directed towards formal literacy, just as they will become directed towards other learning activities. Consequently, there is no such thing as pre-literacy, since there is no especial start for literacy; there can be no 'pre' and no such thing as 'readiness'.

The process of emergent reading starts with visual and aural recognition, as young children learn to 'decode' the physical and social environment surrounding them. Experience, practice and informal teaching serve to help children to accumulate expertise and knowledge; gradually a child's 'reach' extends to manage more varied cues and a wider range of information. Within this context, knowledge accumulates about alphabetic, phonic and print characteristics so that children come to act more independently in moving towards literacy, to the point where they are taught directly.

Development brings about a process of refinement and improvement in the under-pinning knowledge of how words are shaped, constructed and recognised in reading and spelling. This process is gradual, and learners may progress through it at different speeds. As children's literacy skills mature, knowledge and understanding move from alphabetic knowledge to knowledge about syllables and then morphemes. In spelling, children become able to call on their literacy experience to make reasonable predictions as to how a new word may be pronounced and formed. However, for young children who experience potential or actual dyslexia, this process may be curtailed.

As early educational settings increase their expectations of young children's reading, adults who are listening to children read will need to remember that dyslexia is characterised by slow and arduous literacy acquisition. There is likely to be more hesitation, more forgetfulness and more resistance on a child's part, so that an adult needs to remain patient and to make the experience of reading as manageable as possible for a child. New words can be reinforced by using multisensory methods; there is no reason to think that a dyslexic child will remember if they are only told the new word. Areas of text that are too large for a child's comfort can be made smaller by masking with paper or a reading ruler. Also, researchers have found that children's reading can be affected by the crowding of words together, so that increasing the spaces between them promotes reading skill (Zorzi *et al.*, 2012).

Ultimately, a child's success in reading a text depends on it being at a suitable level of difficulty, with a certain amount of challenge so that it is not too easy, but also not too hard. Against this is set the fact that a child may want to tackle a text that is, technically, too difficult because they like the book or are interested in its subject. While such an interest in reading can be encouraged, it is important not to give a dyslexic child a text that is known to be too difficult in the hope that this will motivate them; the opposite may happen.

Emergent writing and writing difficulty

Some co-occurring characteristics have been both proposed and dismissed as being part of a dyslexic profile, but are, nevertheless, associated with dyslexia. Difficulty with writing is one such characteristic. Debate has been complicated by the fact that, in the UK, handwriting difficulty – if not considered as part of dyslexia – has been seen as falling within a diagnosis of dyspraxia (developmental coordination disorder). In the USA, writing difficulty has been known as 'dysgraphia', a term which now may also be found in the UK.

Under the diagnostic criteria published in *DSM-5*, the category of specific learning disorders includes written language, which describes not only handwriting disrupted perhaps to the point of illegibility, but also impairment in written expression. Factors of cognition governing written expression are not physically apparent and may be overlooked in the demand to secure written language skills. A written language disorder is not only a question of letter order or tidiness, but also a question of how someone attempts to organise thoughts and ideas in written form.

Mark-making and early drawing tends to follow a universal developmental pattern, but then cultural factors assert themselves quickly. Early imitations of 'writing' may sometimes be seen in children's drawing, with rows of letter-like symbols incorporated into pictures. Sometimes, signs of a possible graphic difficulty may occur in the mark-making of young children. It may be that a child's graphic development is unusual when compared with that of others; a practitioner might then want to pay particular attention to noticing how a particular child responds to early letter formation.

A practitioner who concludes that there is something unusual in a child's response to early writing will, first of all, need to consider whether this is arising from a question of immaturity of style, or lack of experience, or a physical difference such as a tremor. However, if he or she concludes that written language is not developing as expected, it is important to remember that, in addition to apparent manipulative skills, there may be organisational or cognitive factors to consider. A practitioner in this situation will need to make sure that teaching input is clear, and that letter formation is supported by additional care in teaching and the use of multisensory methods. If concerns continue, referral to an occupational therapist would be indicated.

Emergent spelling and spelling difficulty

Historic approaches to spelling are tenacious. Spellings are viewed as either correct or incorrect and judgements about individuals may be made on that basis, as if spelling was somehow a sign of character. We now understand that spelling emerges; we encourage children to invent and attempt spellings. Even good spellers get some words wrong and it is common for good spellers to try out different versions of a word until they find the one that looks 'right' – this is a strategy that can be encouraged as writers become more knowledgeable and confident.

Our understanding of spelling owes a great deal to efforts to fathom the difficulties experienced by learners with dyslexia. The focus upon phonics that characterises the modern approach to reading and spelling has grown from research regarding the significance of phonological difficulty in dyslexia. Dyslexia specialists teach reading and spelling through systematically structured programmes comprised of phonemes, syllables and morphemes, addressing also syntax, etymology and comprehension. This approach can be found now in mainstream practice, described in Support for Spelling (DCSF, 2010). This programme provides structured objectives and practices for spelling from six years of age (Year 2) onwards.

Spelling is often associated with writing, being seen as the characteristic that enables children to display fluency and maturity in written work. Joshi and Carreker (2009) make the point that spelling is connected to reading, but it is not the reverse of reading. While reading can call on context, and readers can make a good guess at a word by recognising some part of it, spelling requires recollection of all the letters in a word in a correctly ordered sequence. Young children's spelling is often phonetic; spelling may seem to remain at that phase of development for many children who experience actual or potential dyslexia. Spelling difficulty is understood to be a core characteristic of dyslexia, so that even when individuals have learnt to read, spelling remains a problem.

Emergent comprehension and comprehension difficulty

The 'simple view of reading' (Hoover and Gough 1990) has drawn attention to a group of learners who are described as 'poor comprehenders' or as experiencing reading comprehension impairment. Learners with this difficulty are seen as having acceptable word recognition skills, but having problems extracting meaning from the text. However, in practice, there are few learners with this profile; Spencer et al. (2014) identify one per cent in their research of readers from first to third grade. Researchers agree that the likeliest underlying causes of poor comprehension are underlying oral language difficulties and/or reduced vocabulary knowledge; reduced decoding skills may also be a factor (Hulme and Snowling, 2011; Spencer et al., 2014).

In early childhood education, expansion of vocabulary is linked to talking initiatives or asking children to answer questions about a text. However, a technique for developing comprehension known as 'reciprocal teaching' and described by Glynn *et al.* (2006), calling on earlier work by Palinscar and her co-authors, can also be adapted for young children. The technique involves students and teacher taking turns in contributing to the work of under-standing a text that they have all shared. The focus is upon four key areas: a summary of the text content; questions that the text has generated; noting and making clearer any aspects that are difficult to understand; and prediction – saying what might happen next. A practi-tioner could encourage a similar process with young children sharing a prearranged text, ensuring that less confident or less verbal children have the opportunity to respond also. For younger children, this process could be applied to sections of stories that are read or shown to them, progressing to texts that are read together. Since the purpose is comprehension rather than decoding, texts do not need to be too challenging. A child who finds the text more difficult can be helped with it and may be stimulated to master it by the discussion.

Promoting foundational skills

For children who experience actual or possible dyslexia it is valuable to reinforce the building of fundamental skills that will support literacy, even past the point at which formal literacy teaching and learning has begun. For pedagogical intensity and for guiding learning, a prac-titioner or other adult needs to be involved. Such foundational activities would include:

- *developing hearing and listening precision:* through identifying voices, unusual sounds, locating the direction of a voice or sound, counting beats, repeating tunes, songs and rhymes, repeating clapping patterns, filling in a missing word from a song or rhyme; and games such as Simple Simon, where physical instructions are followed;
- *developing articulation of speech sounds:* through singing, talking, reciting, acting, exaggerating the opening of jaws and mouths when doing these activities, speaking loudly and speaking softly, putting more 'up-and-down' into what is being said, and exaggerating this for fun;
- *developing rhythm and beat perception:* through clapping beats and syllables, repeating short beat patterns made up by a leader, such as are made by following children's names: 'Vic-tor-i-a', 'Ry-an'; or favourite food items: 'pizz-a', 'fish-and-chips', 'tan-doo-ri chick-en'; doing these activities with percussion instruments; performing call and response, where two patterns alternate; trying to maintain one pattern against another (a class or group would be divided into two halves, with each half supported by an adult); incorporating these into follow-my-leader games and dances;
- *drawing, painting and modelling:* through continuous availability of resources – paper, paint, felt pens, modelling materials and compounds – in a designated area where they may be made available; drawing/modelling something to help learn or remember a new word; drawing to tell a story;
- *narrating, conversing and using new words:* through news, jokes and retelling of stories; allowing conversations and questions to be open, rather than closed down; making a game of introducing a new word and seeing who can use it during the day or session, reprising it at the end; expecting answers to be in more of a sentence form rather than in single words;
- *finding, matching and recognising items and discriminating between them visually:* through 'finding' games like Hunt the Thimble (or slipper), puzzles, shape-matching

games, games where children have to collect a set or family of items; sorting activities; and the following of simple then compound instructions, e.g. 'Please give me the long red pencil';

- *building, connecting and sequencing activities*: through construction toys, used individually, in pairs or in groups; junk modelling; ordering toys by size, type, colour etc., using both large and small items; drawing or making storyboards; deciding what would be all the steps in a familiar activity, such as feeding a cat, brushing teeth, putting on socks; putting each step into a separate picture and arranging them along a wall, in sequence, perhaps sometimes, intentionally, mixing them up;

- *displaying curiosity and questioning*: through identifying a hidden object by asking questions about it; by asking children to generate questions in talking- or story-time or singing activities, e.g. 'Who has a question about Cinderella?'; acting on the belief that a child who asks a question is entitled to a sensible answer; making sure conversations and questions are not closed down by adults;

- *acting and miming*: through action games and songs; guess-the-mime games; accepting children using their hands, faces and bodies when expressing themselves; adults doing the same, to make a strong point, rather than relying on voices; asking 'Who can show me a picture of (a topic) happening, by acting it?'; accustoming children to act as an audience, watching and learning rather than giggling; encouraging children to act and augment familiar stories and songs; respecting the shyness of children who do not feel comfortable participating;

- *developing faster response times*: by giving children a timer for a small task or game where a practitioner wants to see speed developing, and asking them to try to improve their own performance (rather than pitting children against each other in competitions or races); recognising that if speed goes up, quality may go down, at least in early stages;

- *remembering and recalling*: by working backwards through memories through not accepting 'I don't remember' as an answer, at least not straight away, but instead applying a backward chain technique, e.g. 'Do you remember what you had for dinner today … breakfast today … tea yesterday … dinner yesterday … in the morning before?'; returning to and rehearsing items that children are required to remember, even after time has gone by;

- *asking children to draw or make something of their own choice that they feel will help them to remember*: through having materials available for this to take place; images being chosen by a child, rather than by an adult; adults avoiding making judgements about what they consider to be the relevance of the item or the quality of its execution; reminding children about the item at a later time if they need help to remember;

- *doing things better a second time*: through exercising good judgement about when to suggest this; asking for a special copy of a picture; asking children to repeat a play or building activity and seeing if they could make it even better; asking 'Could it be made better?' and 'What might make it better?'; accepting that some things reach a finishing point and cannot really be improved.

Dyslexia-friendly principles: supporting the development of connectivity

If reduced activation of language/literacy connections is a significant element in dyslexia, then the necessary connections are unlikely to form easily by themselves. In terms of neuroscience, such connections are internal: they are manifestations of brain activity. However, connections made in the physical world create active insights and understanding, establishing new concepts. To consider how we might increase the chances of connectivity when literacy learning takes place, we must maintain a focus on what we know about dyslexia:

- when learners experience dyslexia, connections do not happen easily;
- multisensory techniques help to make connections;
- we cannot teach a rule or an item once and expect to move on; reminding and revisiting is necessary to reinforce and establish connections;
- we need to connect new learning to old learning;
- we can demonstrate connections by linking items in actuality – e.g. by using real strings to connect pictures or objects;
- we need to make learning simple, vivid, memorable and fun, to increase its impact and to increase chances of connectivity.

Dyslexia-friendly practice: 'I begin with M says the ...'

This lesson, used with children at the earliest stages of recognising letter sounds, also helps dyslexic learners by providing entertaining visual aspects in support of phonically-based input. The lesson could be used for word beginnings, endings, or middles. It could also be used to demonstrate a Mind Map® or other graphic representation. In this activity reading, writing, spelling and drawing are moved closer together.

In front of the class or group, the teacher writes up:

I begin with M (or letter of choice) **says the**

s/he then elicits ideas from children by asking for something to eat, for example, or something to drink, an animal, something to wear, something in the house. Children contribute ideas, trying them out against the target sound/letter. The teacher draws the relevant pictures on the board, perhaps to some hilarity ... s/he writes the names of the items underneath. The children copy down the heading, the drawings and the names. Only a few items are required.

It is possible to criticise the idea of copying from a board, the idea of children imitating an adult's drawing, or the idea of sharing ideas rather than children having to originate a word for themselves. However, this is a short, simple, fun lesson that has a positive effect. There is discussion while everyone tries to think of something for each category in turn and while they test out the sound of the words to see if they are right. There is discussion if the target sound falls somewhere other than the beginning, discussion about the drawings and so on. If a child has difficulty copying from the board, or writing words to that standard, they can be given a card to copy, or the words can be written for them to copy, with a practitioner modelling the writing for a child. The number of items can be differentiated – for example, children can be asked to pick three, while children who finish early can go on to do more. Practitioners could develop the activity according to their own requirements.

Information and communication technology: LeapFrog

LeapFrog is a company that has, for some time, produced electronic educational toys for young children. In recent years it has benefited from the advances in technology that have produced tablets and apps. The LeapFrog range of learning toys, learning games and children's computers is considerable, but its tablets (under the LeapPad™ name) have allowed for the development of a wide range of LeapFrog's own educational and play apps.

LeapPad™ devices use a 'closed' system, which means that only its own apps are usable on LeapPad™ machines. The benefit of a closed system is that unwanted material cannot find its way on to a child's tablet. LeapFrog designs its range of products to be available for children aged from a few months up to about eight years of age, with products for the youngest children taking the form of electronic toys rather than tablets.

The LeapFrog company produces a wide range of apps and these have an educational as well as play function; there is a strong focus on early literacy and numeracy skills. The price of LeapFrog apps has been noted as being more expensive than those for iPad or Android operating systems. However, the apps claim to benefit from educational expertise in their production. Reviews for parents, for these and other electronic resources, can be found on www.mumsnet.com and www.geekmummy.com

Learning game: Spaceship – a game to support initial sound/letter recognition

Children form a circle where there is room to run round it outside; a practitioner starts the game by nominating a 'caller'. The children chant 'Girl (or boy) from space, may I chase?'

The caller replies, 'Yes, if your name begins like (e.g.) "bird".' Children with this initial chase the caller round the ring and if he or she is tagged, the tagger becomes the new caller and the person caught goes to the centre, to the 'space ship', which could be a mat, rope boundary, hoops, bench etc. If the caller gets back safely, a practitioner can nominate the next caller.

After a small group of children are in the space ship, a practitioner can call out 'Get ready for launch – the spaceship is going to take off!' All the children, and the practitioner, crouch down and make a whooshing sound as they gradually come upright, raising their arms to represent the ship taking off. The children in the spaceship wave and call 'Goodbye' while the children in the ring wave and call back.

Adapted from McNicholas and McEntee (1991, 2004), no. 9: Teaching Initial Letter – Man or Woman from Space (p. 8).

How can dyslexia be supported in this game?

- Preparation can be done beforehand to check that children all know the initial sound of their own name.

- A child who is uncertain about this can have a little individual work done with them until they are secure with the sound.
- A practitioner can observe the group to see if there is any child who never runs, or who runs every time. If this is the case, they can be nominated as caller to support their correct involvement in the game.
- Using all the letters of the alphabet would not work for this game. It would be better to play a few rounds using the same letters but with different children nominating them. A practitioner can make sure that everyone has a turn, by announcing that they are going to choose a caller.
- A practitioner can steer the game so that everyone has a turn; a potentially dyslexic child can have some individual preparation to make sure they can think of a sound and a word that goes with it for their turn.
- A practitioner can steer the game by giving a child a card with a chosen letter sound on it. This could be extended to focusing the game upon particular letter sounds.
- Playing the game until everyone in a class has had a chance to be caller would be too lengthy; it would be better to repeat the game on different days, making sure everyone has had their turn.
- Collaborative game-playing can be encouraged by asking the whole group to make sure that everyone has a turn, i.e. giving the group some responsibility for this.

Attitude, understanding, technique and empathy: supporting emergent literacy

Practitioners may find that, professionally, they are required to follow strictly structured literacy programmes. Considerations of attitude, understanding, technique and empathy can be used to support their effectiveness:

- *attitude*: being vigilant for emerging signs of a possible difficulty;
- *understanding*: recognising that reading, writing and spelling are interrelated and can be encouraged through a child's interests and engagement;
- *technique*: focusing upon talking to develop children's receptive and expressive language, to help in creating meanings and understanding and to demonstrate knowledge and enthusiasm about texts;
- *empathy*: appreciating that, in teaching and learning, what appears logical and sensible practice to a practitioner may not appear so to a young learner who experiences potential or actual dyslexia.

Recommended reading

1. Hayden, S. and Jordan, E. (2007) *Language for Learning*, NASEN/David Fulton/ Routledge
2. Joshi, M. and Carreker, S. (2009) Spelling: Development Assessment and Instruction, in G. Reid (ed.), *The Routledge Companion to Dyslexia*, Abingdon, Routledge
3. Dockrell, J. and Stuart, M. (2007) *Talking Time*, London, Institute of Education, University of London/Canary Wharf Group PLC

Useful websites

1. www.leapfrog.com
   This is the website for the LeapFrog range of products: toys, tablets and gaming systems and apps. The range of products is listed by age and by type. Placing the cursor on a product opens a quickview tab, which when clicked upon reveals a short demonstration.
2. www.mumsnet.com
   Mumsnet is an award-winning discussion forum for parents. It has grown to provide parents with an important opportunity for their voices to be heard; parents have developed a number of campaigns through the website. Mumsnet's contributors comment on all matters concerning parenting, they provide advice and also provide product reviews. The website carries a number of discussion threads about dyslexia.
3. www.geekmummy.com
   Geekmummy is a blog website. It is the work of Ruth Arnold, who, with the help of her family, explores and assesses new technology. In her Favourite Apps column, Geekmummy reviews apps for babies, toddlers and preschool children. Geekmummy's reports are informative, entertaining and convincing, and the website has won many awards.

MY DYSLEXIA EXPERIENCE: NAVIGATING SCHOOL WITH A DYSLEXIC CHILD

Moving from one's notion of the ideal child to the real one is a common challenge for many parents, but parents of dyslexic children are hit early and hard with the reality that almost everything to do with learning in the early grades is particularly difficult for their children ... My son, Dylan, like many other dyslexic children, went to great lengths to disguise his challenges. He employed his excellent oral vocabulary, sophisticated humour and emotional intelligence to keep us all distracted from the thing that privately shamed and haunted him: Dylan thought he was stupid. (Redford, 2014)

References

Department for Children, Schools and Families (DCSF) (2010) *Support for Spelling*, Nottingham, DCSF

Dockrell, J. and Stuart, M. (2007) *Talking Time*, London, Institute of Education, University of London/Canary Wharf Group PLC

Dooley, C. (2011) The Emergence of Comprehension: A Decade of Research 2000–2010, *International Electronic Journal of Elementary Education*, 4, 1, 169–84

Glynn, T., Wearmouth, J. and Berryman, M. (2006) *Supporting Students with Literacy Difficulties: A Responsive Approach*, Maidenhead, Open University Press

Hayden, S. and Jordan, E. (2007) *Language for Learning*, NASEN/David Fulton/Routledge

Hoover, W. and Gough, P. (1990) The Simple View of Reading, *Reading and Writing: an Interdisciplinary Journal*, 2, 2, 127–60.

Hulme, C. and Snowling, M. (2011) Children's Reading Comprehension Difficulties: Nature, Causes and Treatments, *Current Directions in Psychological Science*, 20, 3, 139–42

Joshi, M. and Carreker, S. (2009) Spelling: Development, Assessment and Instruction, in G. Reid (ed.), *The Routledge Companion to Dyslexia*, Abingdon, Routledge

McNicholas, J. and McEntee, J. (1991, 2004) *Games to Improve Reading Levels*, NASEN/Routledge

Palinscar, A. and Brown, A. (1983) *Reciprocal Teaching of Comprehension-monitoring Activities*, Technical Report No. 269, Champaign, University of Illinois

Perani, D., Saccuman, M., Scifo, P., Anwander, A., Spada, D., Baldori, C., Poloniato, A., Lohmann, G. and Friederici, A. (2011) Neural Language Networks at Birth, *Proceedings of the National Academy of Sciences*, 108, 38, 16056–61

Ramus, F., Marshall, C., Rosen, S. and van der Lely, H. (2013) Phonological Deficits in Specific Language Impairments and Developmental Dyslexia: Towards a Multidimensional Model, *Brain*, 136, 2, 630–45

Redford, K. (2014) *Navigating School with a Dyslexic Child*, New Haven, Yale Center for Dyslexia and Creativity, available online at: http://dyslexia.yale.edu/PAR_NavigatingSchool.html

Spencer, M., Quinn, J. and Wagner, R. (2014) Specific Reading Comprehension Disability: Major Problem, Myth or Misnomer?, *Learning Disabilities Research and Practice*, 29, 1, 3–9

Whitehurst, G. and Lonigan, C. (1998) Child Development and Emergent Literacy, *Child Development*, 69, 3, 848–72

Zorzi, M., Barbiero, C., Facoetti, A., Lonciari, I., Carrozzi, M., Montico, M., Bravar, L., George, F., Pech-Georgel, C. and Ziegler, J. (2012) Extra-large Letter Spacing Improves Reading in Dyslexia, *Proceedings of the National Academy of Sciences (PNAS)*, 109, 28, 11455–9

Chapter 8

Dyslexia and developing reading, writing and spelling

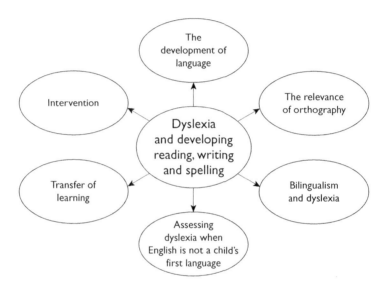

Good practice points

For good practice we need to:

1. use the alphabet arc, embedded letters and mouth shapes to develop alphabetic knowledge;
2. develop phonemic knowledge by teaching blending of sounds and segmenting;
3. give time to phonological aspects known to be difficult for dyslexic children, e.g. b/d, p/q confusion, vowel identification;
4. provide additional help and manage/record this through provision mapping;
5. encourage awareness of books by providing, using and reading aloud well-illustrated texts with small amounts of clear writing on each page.

Phonological abilities

Phonological abilities are concerned with being able to perceive, recognise and apply the sounds of speech as they are used in words. For educators, the particular importance of phonology lies in its relevance for reading and writing. The power of the present emphasis on phonological learning comes in part from the highly researched understanding that phonological difficulty or deficit is a core feature of reading disability or dyslexia, especially in the English language (Hulme and Snowling, 2009). The intensity of research in this area has led to finely detailed understandings, finely tuned differences in terminology and some overlapping constructs:

Phonological awareness: the ability to focus on sounds in speech rather than meanings; it begins early in life with infant responses to sounds. Phonological awareness does not relate directly to reading, writing and spelling, but, in a phonically based approach to literacy, it precedes them. Phonological awareness includes being able to hear separate words, the syllables within words, and the sounds within syllables and rhymes.

Phonemic awareness: an aspect of phonological awareness. The term describes a focus upon phonemes – that is, the individual sounds that make up a word.

Phonological sensitivity: the increase in phonological awareness in young children, as shown by their ability to accomplish phonological tasks. Phonological sensitivity increases with development, and is seen as an indicator of later reading skill. Research has identified phonological sensitivity in children as young as two or three (Lonigan *et al.*, 1998).

Phonological processing: the interpretation and use of phonological information, identifying sounds and recognising them in spoken words.

Phonological skills: this term represents the activities that individuals carry out in manipulating phonological information. These manipulations take place when learners take part in word play, when they learn to read, write and spell and when they respond to phonics assessments. Lists of phonological skills vary; they may include: blending syllables or splitting words into syllables, segmenting words into phonemes, recognising and making rhymes, identifying initial sounds or swapping them between words, blending sounds into words, or removing phonemes from words. Each of these holds pitfalls for children who experience potential or actual dyslexia. Moats and Tolman outline a progression in early phonological skills:
- word awareness
- rhyme and alliteration in word play
- syllable awareness
- onset and rime
- phoneme awareness (Moats and Tolman, 2009).

In linguistics, 'onset' is a syllable's initial sound; 'rime' is the part of the syllable consisting of its vowel and any consonants following.

Phonemes: these are the different sounds that go to make up a word and 'phonemic awareness' focuses upon a learner's discrimination and perception of these. Phonemes do not always correspond to single letters; sometimes a sound is made up of two, three or four letters – differences can be subtle. Being able to identify the separate phonemes in a word is not always easy; children find it easier to identify syllables than phonemes. A child who experiences potential or actual dyslexia will need considerably more tailored input than other children in order to develop secure phonological skills. Such input will require quality in the form of dyslexia-aware pedagogy, but will also require quantity in the form of additional, dyslexia-aware practice.

Experience suggests that children with phonological difficulties may sometimes be missing fundamental information about sounds, letters, or grammatical usage because it has been harder for children to internalise them and the teaching has moved on. Even when children are older and teaching has advanced to more complex matters it is worth checking whether all the necessary sound and letter knowledge is in place. If some of this knowledge is absent, then increased, systematic intensity of teaching input and increased responsiveness on the part of practitioners are required in order to provide the missing knowledge and link it to existing, secure knowledge.

Phonics

The term 'phonics' has come to describe the approach to literacy that depends on being able to recognise the phonemes in speech sounds and relate them to letters in the alphabet. Knowing these, a reader is expected to be able to discern and blend them, both to identify a word in reading, and to represent it in writing, via spelling. 'Systematic' phonics programmes have been used to help dyslexic learners acquire literacy since the development, in the 1930s, of the Orton–Gillingham method. This approach makes use of sequential, cumulative, frequently-rehearsed knowledge about how words are structured, pronounced and written. Programmes of this kind now lead literacy teaching. They focus upon 'synthetic' phonics, which describes the bringing together of sounds in order to understand how they will be read, spelt and written.

Modern, phonics-based literacy teaching has its own characteristics. There is no single agreed sequence of phonics instruction and sounds are not necessarily taught alphabetically; they may have to be linked separately to alphabetic knowledge. In addition, one of the expectations of present-day phonics teaching is that it will be carried out briskly. This is generally taken as meaning teaching one phoneme each day, with the whole range of phonemes being accomplished within the first year of formal literacy learning. A demand by some that phonics should be taught 'first, fast and only' has been moderated by serving practitioners who accept the value of 'first and fast', but who also retain the right to use other methods where they deem them to be appropriate (Walker *et al.*, 2013). These other methods include engaging children's imagination and stimulating them to read, through an appreciation of books and other texts.

Teachers in England have begun to concentrate efforts on the decoding of pseudo-words, as well as real words, in order to meet the challenge of phonics testing (Walker *et al.*, 2014). This may prove to be an example of the greater intensity of teaching needed for children who experience potential or actual dyslexia. However, there have been criticisms of the phonics-led approach; one such criticism has focused upon its effect on young learners who experience potential or actual dyslexia. This has given rise to a question as to whether it helps or hinders dyslexic children to concentrate so much time and effort on the particular learning that they find most problematic, tying them to a repetitive routine in which success is always difficult. A further question is how 'brisk pace' can be expected when children experience slower processing speeds, through no fault of their own. There is an expectation that most children will manage this learning and that those who do not will receive enhanced input to help them to keep pace, but, since dyslexia encompasses a range, for some children there will be considerable difficulties.

Blending sounds

The purpose of systematic, synthetic phonics work is to enable children to be able to work out new words when they meet them and to transfer their phonics learning into new spellings. This approach depends on being able to blend sounds by sliding them together. Byrne describes this process as 'coarticulation', representing 'the overlapping of articulatory gestures' (Byrne, 2002: 35).

When the blending of phonemes is discussed in the teaching of literacy, there is little explanation as to how this takes place. Sometimes children are taught to speak the phonemes faster and faster, as if somehow the sounds will then run together. This does not really happen; n-a-p spoken quickly still remains n-a-p. For this to turn into a word depends on a child's intuitive leap, perhaps making use of a visual cue or adult modelling, such as, 'nuh-ah-puh: nap. Now you say it.' Accurate blending is better served by elongating the sounds until they run together, as a single, long sound.

Vowels are important in this process. While vowel combinations may have different pronunciations, for young children the focus is on two aspects: the long sound (the name of the letter) and the short sound (the sound it makes). For clarity, we need to teach each sound for vowels, distinguishing between the letter name and its sound. It is necessary also to teach consonants not only as letter names but as sounds, making it very clear which version is which, because often children will have been taught the alphabet's letter names before they start formal schooling and confusion needs to be avoided.

Consonants are sometimes sounded and sometimes not. Educators are keen to emulate the actual phonic sound of consonants rather than to add a vowel to them, as often happens ('nuh-a-puh'). However, this can result in a collection of sounds that are difficult to pronounce, to model and to copy, being made with the mouth but not, as such, with a voice. Mouth shapes can help with this and examples of correct phonic pronunciation can be found on the World Wide Web.

Blending by extending or elongating sounds needs to be modelled by an adult, demonstrating simple consonant-vowel-consonant words or syllables. The initial sound is held and voiced while the reader works out the next sound, for example 'nnnnnn-aaaaaa' – and then the final sound is brought in, sliding each sound into the next on the same, sounded note: 'nnnnnn-aaaaaa-pppppp'. This way the sounds actually run together. A speech exercise that could help to hold sounds until the next one slides into place is to stretch all the vowels as if to make a word ('aeiou'), exaggerating the mouth shapes and sounds to make them clear.

In blending, practitioners will need to use their judgement about prompting. However, it seems unlikely that prompting with phoneme *content* will interfere with the *process* of learning to blend. Once the sounds are in place, the blend can be spoken more and more quickly until the word is secure. Gagen (2007) suggests that preparation can be made for blending work by familiarising children through verbal games and sound activities; she also recommends that a child takes a breath before beginning to blend sounds.

An important adjunct to the blending of sounds is the activity of segmenting. This involves breaking up words into syllables, and syllables into phonemes, in order to recognise how to read a word and, later, to write it. MacKay's Make and Break technique recommends making a word from its component letters, segmenting it into syllables, sounding out the syllables while recombining these to build the word again, then mixing up the letters before building them into the word once more, saying the letter names in the process (MacKay, 2012: 62). Practice of segmenting can be aided by putting single words onto cards in large print and letting children cut them up with scissors. At a later date, drawn lines can be substituted for actual cuts.

Developing phonemic and alphabetic knowledge

Ehri's (2014) review of literacy research highlights specific ways in which young children may be aided to acquire early alphabetic and phonic knowledge. These include the use of embedded mnemonics, also known as embedded letters, and the use of pictures to show the shapes that mouths make when pronouncing letter sounds and names.

Embedded mnemonics/letters are those in which the shape of the letter is incorporated into a picture of an object, with the object drawn in the shape of the letter. The name of the object starts with the letter shown. This is more effective than drawing an object for the letter which does not follow the letter shape. With embedded mnemonics/letters, children take fewer attempts to master the letters and remember them for longer. Ehri considers that:

> Embedded mnemonics can be used to teach harder-to-learn correspondences such as the short vowel sounds of A, E, I, O and U: the consonants Y, W and H; and the hard sounds for C/k, and G/g, all letters whose names do not contain their sounds.
>
> (Ibid.: 14)

A useful example of embedded letters can be found in the work of Jan Shandera at Cardinal Concepts (thecardinalconcepts.com).

Figure 8.1 Examples of embedded mnemonics/letters

© Jan Shandera

Mouth pictures. Ehri points out that practitioners will usually ask learners to notice the sounds of letters. However, her research shows that phonic and alphabetic learning can be aided by showing learners the shapes that are made by mouths when sounds are pronounced or letters named. Learners copy the mouth shapes, becoming involved in the look of the mouth shapes, the feel of them and the sense of expulsion of air, in addition to the sounds and letters themselves. This multisensory approach increases the impact so that the letter-sound is remembered better than by sound alone. The author points out: 'Whereas sounds are ephemeral and disappear as soon as they are heard, mouth positions are tangible and can be felt, viewed in a mirror, and analyzed by learners' (ibid.: 10).

The drawings of mouth shapes below are by animated-film artist David Bromfield (http://vimeo.com/anibromation). They were not originally intended for language and literacy use, but as aide memoires for animators. The drawings can guide educators in drawing or demonstrating mouth shapes for themselves.

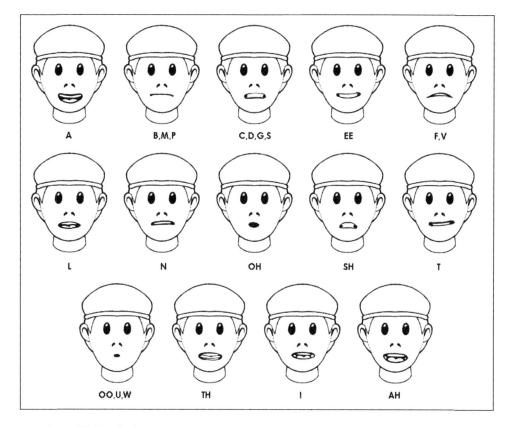

Figure 8.2 Mouth shapes

© David Bromfield

Developing reading

With the current emphasis on phonics, Compton *et al.* (2014) consider that the teaching of reading has moved too far away from its theoretical foundations and that, in order to help dyslexic individuals, we should consider what skilled readers do. The authors identify two processes – those of word-level reading and comprehension, corresponding to Hoover and Gough's (1990) 'simple view of reading' – but see them as supporting each other.

The authors make the point that skilled decoding of the phonemes in a word is not sufficient for it to become a 'known' word. They believe that skilled reading involves knowledge and application of context, which in turn supports decoding. They wish to see specific, focused 'orthographic-phonological' (decoding) teaching and learning carried out alongside word-specific mastery that extends vocabulary, embeds it in context and helps readers to identify new words.

Following Ziegler and Goswami's (2005) Psycholinguistic Grain Size theory, the authors consider that literacy in English requires learners to have a variety of ways of building words, including, besides phonic decoding, recognition of larger patterns (such as syllables, morphemes, prefixes and suffixes); they also need to be able to recognise whole words. They believe that whole-word, contextualised reading needs to be taught in tandem with decoding strategies. Furthermore, they affirm that new reading materials should make use of words that have greatest general application of spelling and the greatest transferability of context. In this way, they seek to promote a literacy learning process that maximises both decoding and contextual (comprehension) approaches. In the absence of such new materials, lists of frequently used syllables, prefixes, suffixes, morphemes or word-roots can be found via World Wide Web research. This enables practitioners to construct their preferred shortlists, focusing upon words that include these elements and making a teaching point of their transferability.

Developing spelling and writing

The English early years Foundation Stage descriptor for 'writing' states that:

> [children] use their phonic knowledge to write words in ways which match their spoken sounds. They also write some irregular common words. They write simple sentences which can be read by themselves and others. Some words are spelt correctly and others are phonetically plausible.
>
> (Department for Education, 2014: 11)

There is a significant amount of ground to cover before this level of skill is established for a dyslexic child. The written forms of speech sounds are known as graphemes; Moats (2005) identifies over 250 graphemes in the English language, some of them having more than one pronunciation. There is not a complete one-to-one correspondence between phonemes and graphemes, so there is plenty of scope for difficulty, especially if a child is not secure in his or her phonemic knowledge.

Young children may have been shown how to make their name before attending early years settings and there may be a need for gentle changes in early writing habits in order to facilitate the cursive writing that is to follow. Of more concern for children with potential or actual dyslexia is the matter of letter confusion or reversal. This has been perceived commonly as a characteristic of dyslexia; in fact, it is a characteristic of delayed development of writing, consistent with a developmental view of dyslexia. Most children grow out of this as they become more skilled at writing, but children with dyslexia may continue this confusion throughout their lives, except when they deliberately focus upon the correct form.

Children with dyslexia who are using the Roman alphabet often confuse letters that have ascenders (b and d) and, similarly, letters with descenders (p and q). They may also confuse vowels with each other, since most vowels have similarly rounded shapes. Tackling b/d confusion is a familiar matter for practitioners, and many practitioners will be familiar with the 'bed' mnemonic. However, this may not prevent confusion. Practitioners are seeing this from the point of view of familiarity – they already know what it says. To help young children we need to understand that they may look at b and d, or p and q, and see no difference at all between them. A different approach is required.

There are puzzles that present two pictures and invite the viewer to find the differences between them. At first the pictures look the same, and then we start to scrutinise the detail, moving from one to the other, comparing them until we find a difference. We repeat the process until we find them all, and at this point we can see the differences clearly; our understanding of the pictures has changed. We can emulate this with two letters that get confused, inviting children to look closely and see what is the same and what is different about them. This involves close scrutiny of differences that are minor and obvious to adults, but this letter knowledge can be helped by the fact that mouth shapes for the sounds are different and the letter formation is different. To dwell on b/d differences in this way may take more time than we plan to devote to two graphemes alone. Nevertheless, where it is known that these are likely to cause problems, it is worth spending the time.

One practitioner known to the author tackles b/d confusion by teaching 'b' kinaesthetically. She asks a child to make a fist with their left hand, index finger pointing forward, to shape the letter 'b'. She believes that there is no point in making 'b' with the left hand and 'd' with the right because it does not prevent confusion. When 'b' is secure, then 'd' becomes 'the other one'; this raises an interesting point. As practitioners we may feel a need to be 'completists', telling children about b *and* d, p *and* q, here *and* hear and so on. It may be more effective to acknowledge in early stages that there are two (or more) possibilities, or two letters that look alike, but to concentrate on one. The remainder then has an identity as the 'other one' and we can teach that. The task of sorting out which one to use becomes a target for teaching in its own right.

Because there is such a difference between phonemes and graphemes in the English language, mnemonics are often used to help a child to remember a spelling. This can be helpful, especially when the mnemonic, such as 'an island is land', can be incorporated into a picture. There are many lists of mnemonics available on the World Wide Web, but mnemonics do not suit everyone. Many children find them helpful, but a responsive teacher will not assume that this will always be the case. He or she will watch carefully to see whether a child finds it just as difficult to remember a mnemonic as to remember a spelling.

Dyslexia-aware principles: provision mapping

Significant differences in literacy acquisition become clearer as the years of early education progress and this should reasonably lead to increased pedagogical efforts. Provision mapping can be used to manage additional input, to keep track of it and to decide what to do next. The provision offered by different settings to help develop literacy skills is likely to vary, and some may not see literacy as the business of early years provision. However, the early years Foundation Stage descriptors expect the following:

> *Reading:* children read and understand simple sentences. They use phonic knowledge to decode regular words and read them aloud accurately. They also read some common irregular words. They demonstrate understanding when talking with others about what they have read.
>
> (Department for Education, 2014: 11)

This can be deconstructed to reveal about 15 separate targets; any and all of these can present difficulties to children with actual or possible dyslexia.

A dyslexia-aware practitioner will need to identify which of these skills are presenting difficulty and consider what more can be done in terms of what is available for their setting. Additional support may be outlined in a provision map, to be held in the records of the school or setting. The aim is to know who is receiving additional help and the nature of the help, and to be able to increase support as needed. The support process can start anywhere, according to need. A time limit can be set on an intervention, such as a number of weeks or a term, and, at its conclusion, an evaluation of the intervention's success can take place, so as to identify routes for progression. Provision mapping software is available for computerised record-keeping purposes.

Spring term 2015	Classroom assistant/ volunteer sits with child in small group	Reading heard 5 times per week, including twice by teacher	10 mins' practice daily in targeted literacy skill	20 mins' individual lesson, 2–3 times per week	One 30–40 min. individual lesson per week, withdrawn from teaching room
Ben	X				
Sarah			X		
Jon					X
Meg		X			
Sami				X	

Figure 8.3 An example of a simple provision map supporting literacy

Dyslexia-aware practice: alphabet arc

The alphabet arc is a central dyslexia-teaching technique. The aim is for students to be able to construct the alphabet correctly, but it can then be used as a teaching tool. Three-dimensional letters of wood or plastic are employed; if wooden letters are used the vowels can be coloured

Figure 8.4 An alphabet arc

to make them more visible; the letter 'y' can be half-coloured to demonstrate that sometimes it is used as a vowel and sometimes not. Some people like to add pictures.

Often, practitioners will start by placing the letter 'n' at the top, in the centre, representing the nose in the centre of a face, but there is no set method of proceeding. Kelly and Phillips (2011) recommend placing 'mn' in the centre, as the central letters in the alphabet, with 'a' and 'z' to show the end markers. Hornsby *et al.* (2006) recommend teaching the letters in three groups: a–g, h–o, then p–z. In contrast, Broomfield (2004) recommends constructing the arc in four sections: a–d, e–m, n–r and s–z. These latter divisions correspond to another classic dyslexia-teaching technique, wherein alphabetical ordering is taught by dividing the dictionary into four sections and then working within each section until a child is familiar with it. This reduces the number of letters that a dyslexic child has to manage at a time.

The arc may not progress in linear fashion; at first, a child may need to double check and move letters around until satisfied. However it is composed, it is important that a child eventually learns to construct the arc accurately. When employing the arc as a teaching tool, letters are pulled out and used for a focus, perhaps in building words or rhymes, or in alphabetical ordering. The arc may stay on a desk as a memory aid, or be put away.

Information and communication technology: Reading Eggs and Mathseeds

Reading Eggs and Mathseeds are programs produced by Blake eLearning, an Australian company. Reading Eggs focuses upon early literacy (3–7 years) and Mathseeds upon numeracy (3–6 years). In addition, there is a literacy program for older readers, Reading Eggspress (7–13 years). The programs have features that young learners would find enjoyable – animations, songs, rewards and avatars – and the teaching content is delivered through game-like activities. There is a wide range of materials and resources in the schemes; materials are designed to provide steps in the learning process. Reading Eggs and Mathseeds are noteworthy among the range of available programs because their visuals are of good quality and not overcrowded; such features can be supportive for learners who experience actual or potential dyslexia. The programs are available for Android and 'i' operating systems, and can operate at school or family level. There are subscription costs, but there is a free trial also available through the websites (http://readingeggs.co.uk/ and http://mathseeds.co.uk).

Learning game: small word challenge

Dyslexic adults sometimes say that small, similar-looking words catch them out.

A practitioner can prepare for this game by focusing teaching on three small words that look and/or sound similar – for example, in/on/an, go/so/no, is/as/us, or any three words that share a similarity. Children are in groups of three and the target words are on cards, face down on the table. Children take it in turns to extract one card and look at it secretly. At a signal from the practitioner the other cards are turned over and the child holding the card challenges the others is to say which one is missing, saying 'What's my word?' When the word is correctly identified, it goes back on the table. The children completing that round of the challenge put their hands up and the practitioner checks ('What was your word?').

As recognition and discrimination increases, the number of words can be increased and the small words mixed, with more variety. The number of children in a group could be increased, or a time limit imposed.

With practice the identification may become speedy, so that no verbal challenge is needed. This would be a sign that the game could move on in complexity.

Adapted from McNicholas and McEntee (1991, 2004), no. 8: Auditory Recall – Remember the Word (p. 7).

How can dyslexia be supported in this game?

- A potentially dyslexic child can learn from peers identifying the small words.
- A potentially dyslexic child can be prepared beforehand with input identifying the small words.
- Using three small words and placing children in groups of three means each child can take a turn; a dyslexic child gets the same chance to control the game and challenge as non-dyslexic peers.
- When a potentially dyslexic child is the challenger, they have the opportunity to take more time look at their word and think about it, which increases their chance of retention.
- A practitioner can check whether everyone has taken a turn in hiding a word; if some children have missed out, s/he can nominate them – a practitioner has the right to control the game for maximum learning.

Attitude, understanding, technique, empathy: developing literacy

Thanks to the efforts of skilled adults and children's own study efforts, most children who have regular schooling learn to read, write and spell to functional levels. Children who find this particularly difficult can be helped by discerning practitioners:

- *attitude*: being patient in guiding readers and responding to their individual needs in finding ways to help them;

- *understanding*: appreciating that some children need greater intensity of input, so that literacy teaching needs to be clearer, more stimulating and more precise;
- *technique*: having a repertoire of strategies, applied in a systematic, consistent way, such as: alphabet arc; embedded letters; mouth shapes; blending techniques and segmenting;
- *empathy*: being aware that reading aloud, writing in front of the class, spelling tests, or anything that singles out a child who struggles with literacy, may have a significant negative impact upon that child. Empathic practitioners find another way.

Recommended reading

1. Goouch, K. and Lambrith, A. (2011) *Teaching Early Reading and Phonics*, London, SAGE
2. Ehri, L. (2014) Orthographic Mapping in the Acquisition of Sight Word Reading, Spelling and Vocabulary Learning, *Scientific Studies of Reading*, 18, 5–21
3. Carroll, J., Bowyer-Crane, C., Duff, F., Hulme, C. and Snowling, M. (2011) *Developing Language and Literacy*, Chichester, John Wiley and Sons

Useful websites

1. http://thecardinalconcepts.com
    The Cardinal Concepts is the name of Jan Shandera's website. It is based in the USA and calls on Jan Shandera's substantial experience as a teacher specialising in the field of literacy and dyslexia. The website offers a range of useful materials for sale, such as the syllable sliders and the embedded letters materials, in different formats. All the materials are designed for preschool children and for early years home and school use.
2. http://www.ling.upenn.edu/
    This is the website for the Reading Road, an illustrated literacy aid from the University of Pennsylvania Department of Linguistics (2009). The sound blending process is described and illustrated effectively here.
3. http://www.readingrockets.org/
    The Reading Rockets website offers broadcasts, online services, free resources and downloads and reports of reading research. The website aims to meet the needs of parents, practitioners and anyone who is interested in helping children learn to read.

MY DYSLEXIA EXPERIENCE: b AND d CONFUSION

Even now, I get b and d confused. When I have time to think, the 'bed' idea is useful because I have an image in my head, but when I read fast or when I am not totally concentrating, or I am tired or stressed, I still can get them mixed up. (Dyslexic adult)

References

Broomfield, H. (2004) *Overcoming Dyslexia Resource Book 1*, London, Whurr. Includes photocopiable resources

Byrne, B. (2002) The Process of Learning to Read: A Framework for Integrating Research and Educational Practice, in R. Stainthorp and P. Tomlinson (eds), *Learning and Teaching Reading*, Leicester, British Psychological Society

Carroll, J., Bowyer-Crane, C., Duff, F., Hulme, C. and Snowling, M. (2011) *Developing Language and Literacy*, Chichester, John Wiley and Sons

Compton, D., Miller, A., Elleman, A. and Steacy, L. (2014) Have We Forsaken Reading Theory in the Name of 'Quick Fix' Interventions for Children With Reading Disability?, *Scientific Studies of Reading*, 18, 55–73

Department for Education (2014) *Statutory Framework for the Early Years Foundation Stage*, London, DfE

Ehri, L. (2014) Orthographic Mapping in the Acquisition of Sight Word Reading, Spelling and Vocabulary Learning, *Scientific Studies of Reading*, 18, 5–21

Gagen, M. (2007) *Blending Explained: Why Smooth Blending is Important to Reading Development and How to Help Students Develop the Ability to Smoothly Blend Sounds Together When Reading*, available online at: http://www.righttrackreading.com

Goouch, K. and Lambrith, A. (2011) *Teaching Early Reading and Phonics*, London, SAGE

Hoover, W. and Gough, P. (1990) The Simple View of Reading, *Reading and Writing: An Interdisciplinary Journal*, 2, 2, 127–60

Hornsby, B., Frear, S. and Pool J. (2006) *Alpha to Omega Teacher's Handbook* (6th edn), Harlow, Heinemann/Dyslexia Action

Hulme, C. and Snowling, M. (2009) *Developmental Disorders of Language Learning and Cognition*, Malden, Wiley-Blackwell

Kelly, K. and Phillips, S. (2011) *Teaching Literacy to Learners with Dyslexia*, London, SAGE

Lonigan, C. Burgess, S., Anthony, J. and Barker, T. (1998) Development of Phonological Sensitivity in 2- to 5-Year-Old Children, *Journal of Educational Psychology*, 90, 2, 294–311

MacKay, N. (2012) *Removing Dyslexia as a Barrier to Achievement* (3rd edn), Wakefield, SEN Marketing (www.senbooks.co.uk)

McNicholas, J. and McEntee, J. (1991, 2004) *Games to Improve Reading Levels*, NASEN/Routledge

Moats, L. (2005) *How Spelling Supports Reading*, available online at: http://www.readingrockets.org

Moats, L. and Tolman, C. (2009) The Development of Phonological Skills (citing Moats, l. and Tolman, C. (2009) *Language Essentials for Teachers of Reading and Spelling (LETRS): The Speech Sounds of English: Phonetics, Phonology, and Phoneme Awareness (Module 2)*. Boston: Sopris West) Arlington, VA, Reading Rockets, available online at: http://www.readingrockets.org

Walker, M., Bartlett, S., Betts, H., Sainsbury, M. and Mehta, P. (2013) *Evaluation of the Phonics Screening Check: First Interim Report*, London, Department for Education/National Foundation for Educational Research (NFER)

Walker, M., Bartlett, S., Betts, H., Sainsbury, M. and Worth, J. (2014) *Phonics Screening Check Evaluation (second research report)*, London, National Foundation for Educational Research (NFER)

Ziegler, J. and Goswami, U. (2005) Reading Acquisition, Developmental Dyslexia, and Skilled Reading Across Languages: A Psycholinguistic Grain Size Theory, *Psychological Bulletin*, 131, 1, 3–29

Chapter 9

Developing maths and science skills in the presence of dyslexia

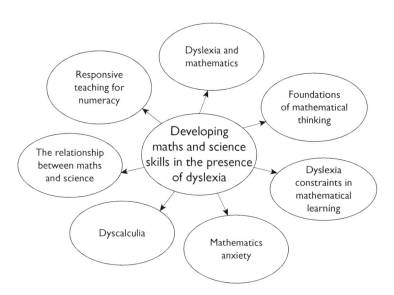

Good practice points

For good practice we need to:

1. keep number work clear, uncrowded and easy to read;
2. use multisensory methods and apparatus for number work, for as long as it helps children;
3. observe children's arithmetical processing in order to gain information about how they learn;
4. take time to make sure that basic maths and science concepts are understood securely and used accurately;
5. work through the correct process when a child makes errors rather than just correcting them.

Dyslexia and mathematics

Research into the genetics and neuroscience of arithmetical/mathematical difficulty is ongoing; there is debate as to whether arithmetical/mathematical difficulty is itself part of a dyslexia profile. Some feel that children with dyslexia always experience mathematical difficulties at some level; others maintain that while there can be an overlap of literacy and numeracy difficulties, they are not necessarily present together all the time. Neurological areas for number are not necessarily the same as those concerned with literacy, although research suggests that there is some genetic overlap between reading and mathematics difficulty (Marino *et al.*, 2011). Furthermore, neurological changes can take place during a lifetime; Butterworth *et al.* (2011) describe the plasticity in a learner's brain which enables mathematical processing to take place in different areas and which can change over time.

There are arguments as to whether there is a separate, identifiable mathematics disability, generally given the name 'developmental dyscalculia', and this gives rise to the question of whether a learner may experience both dyslexia and dyscalculia concurrently. However, the trajectory for understanding of mathematics difficulty or disability has lagged behind that for literacy and much remains to be done. Whether or not the term 'dyscalculia' is used, there are difficulties with definition. Just as with literacy, issues of teaching and learning are raised as complicating factors; confidence plays a large part. The concept of 'mathematics fear' is well explored in the literature as a cause of mathematics failure – far more so, at present, than is mathematics disability or dyscalculia.

The foundations of mathematical thinking

Cognitive characteristics involving a sense of number are considered to have an evolutionary purpose. It is a fundamental survival skill to be able to comprehend numbers of things, whether they are edible items, landscape features or threats. Analysis of visual patterns is also a survival skill. Even very young children have a sense of number, known as 'numerosity', that enables them to recognise small groups of dots or items and to recognise which out of two groups is bigger.

Early number processing focuses, for the most part, upon arithmetic, although arithmetic is only one part of mathematics. Young children will use an empirical style of arithmetic for counting, sharing, subtracting and building up sets of items. Butterworth *et al.* (ibid.) point out that the activation of numbers and number facts through memory also triggers a sense of the meaning of those numbers; calculations do not become completely abstract.

When young children start to process numbers they map items onto their fingers. Counting begins with fingers and may continue that way for a long time, even into adulthood. Butterworth and his co-authors note that this mapping process is the foundation of arithmetical processing. They state: 'neuroscience research suggests that rather than address isolated conceptual gaps, remediation should build the foundation number concepts first' (ibid.: 1051).

These foundational concepts include set enumeration and comparison. To support enumeration, it may be argued that counting on fingers should be encouraged as a positive practice by practitioners, until they are certain that counting is both accurate and secure.

Butterworth and his co-authors consider that teaching should follow the neuroscience, understanding that numerical processing triggers a meaning for numbers and that difficulties lie in recognising and comparing the magnitude of arrays of dots or objects, counting and mapping numbers to quantities. Apparatus such as Cuisenaire rods, Dienes mathematical materials and abacus, have a long pedigree in attaching meaning to numbers and numerical processes. Today, computer programs can incorporate the same kinds of activities, and can include self-checking and feedback functions that do not rely on an adult's input.

Many children will have had valuable practice in counting and writing numerals at home. As with literacy, even very young children bring with them different skills, experience and expectations as they move towards a more formal education. However, children who have learnt to 'do sums' at home from older adults may have been taught using methods and styles no longer used in primary schools. For this reason it would be good practice for schools to offer training to parents, grandparents and caregivers in the styles and programmes of arithmetical activity followed by the school, or, alternatively, to avoid asking for home activities that depend on computation.

Dyslexia constraints in mathematics learning

Learning to write includes learning to form numbers. Arithmetic using apparatus is gradually replaced by arithmetical notation; figures become increasingly important. At this stage, and setting aside issues of possible specific mathematical difficulty, there are a number of ways in which dyslexia can constrain early arithmetical/mathematical learning. The same sort of errors that start to appear in written work may also play a part in number work. New terminology begins to be used, and there may be confusion when a 'conversational' style switches to mathematical language and the use of symbols; a dyslexic child may not be able to see the differences between +, x, ÷, or –.

Even if a child has understood the concepts and remembered them, there may be errors of sequencing, alignment and number reversals. Any of these may make arithmetical processing appear incorrect. Meehan (2013) describes the detail that may need to be in place to enable a child to remember numbers:

> The child may think that a two is like a swan and an eight is like a snowman – and the image of a swan and a snowman holding hands may make the number 10 come to mind more readily than saying the words for a student who is not retaining the number bond by conventional means. (Ibid.: 62)

As with literacy, arithmetic is taught by people who are already skilled in this area. To them, the progression of numerical steps seems obvious and logical. A practitioner may not be aware that something they regard as 'crystal clear' may be incomprehensible to their student. A practitioner may be at ease with a linear, stepwise, logical, presentation of mathematical concepts without appreciating that a dyslexic learner may approach these from a different perspective. Mathematics pedagogy looks for understanding of, and conformance to, correct procedures, in a stepwise progression which may not suit some dyslexic learners.

Mathematics anxiety

A child with or without dyslexia may experience the above difficulties and, if such difficulties occurred repeatedly, it would be very easy for a child to lose confidence. This can escalate into mathematics anxiety, which is a fear of mathematics and anything to do with it. The main reason for this anxiety is 'cumulative negative experiences' (Vukovic *et al.*, 2013). Vukovic and her co-authors find that this can begin in early childhood.

A practitioner needs to be alert to this and to find ways to help. A spoken explanation merely compounds anxiety and bafflement; a frightened learner will have given up in despair by a practitioner's second sentence, and may pretend to understand in the hope that the teacher will stop talking and go away. A vicious circle is created of inadequate understanding, fear of a teacher's (negative) attention, poor skill, insufficient practice and failure to thrive mathematically. As with literacy, a learner who is weak in this skill will find it more arduous and consequently achieve less, and do less practice, than others. He or she will have considerably less of the reinforcement provided by success and, consequently, less confidence. If a learner's calculations are correct they may not know why, but just be relieved that for the moment they are safe.

Mathematics anxiety is not restricted to classrooms alone and may be experienced by practitioners as well as by pupils. However, numeracy teaching can do more in order to become as accessible as possible, in the same way that we would now expect of literacy. There are many numeracy materials, guides and programs aimed at helping young learners to increase their number skills, available through the World Wide Web. As with dyslexia, materials supporting learners with arithmetical difficulty, or dyscalculia, will also benefit other learners and a multisensory approach will support this learning.

Dyscalculia

Specific learning difficulties in both numeracy and literacy are manifested as failure to make progress in the face of skilled teaching. *DSM-5* criteria recognise mathematics disorder, identified through low scores in psychometric assessments. There is no agreed cut-off point, but the expectation is that the difficulty would be significant and persistent over time. Like dyslexia, arithmetical/mathematical disability can be inherited and it has a similar level of incidence – Butterworth and his co-authors put this at 5–7 per cent of the population.

As with dyslexia, the issues are concerned with whether dyscalculia is the same as other numeracy difficulty, but in a more extreme form, whether it is as aspect of, or influenced by, dyslexia, or whether it represents a 'single core deficit' (Butterworth *et al.*, 2011: 1049). Although they consider that all dyslexic learners experience arithmetical/mathematical difficulty at some level, Evans *et al.* (2014) do not rule out the existence, possibly co-occurrence, of a separate, independent difficulty in the form of mathematics disorder (dyscalculia).

Szűchs and Goswami offer a broad definition that calls upon thoughts, feelings and experiences of mathematics disability. They frame their understanding of dyscalculia in a way that rules out the impact of mathematics fear: 'We define it as persistently weak mathematical performance of developmental origin, related to the weakness of some kind(s) of cognitive function(s) and/or representation(s); appearing when concurrent motivation to study mathematics and access to appropriate mathematics education is normal' (Szűchs and Goswami, 2013: 33).

For learners with this difficulty, numbers are not perceived as having meaning in the same way that they are for other learners. Dyscalculic learners '[d]o not intuitively grasp the size of a number and its value relative to other numbers' (Butterworth *et al.*, 2011: 1050). Ronit Bird describes the empirical characteristics of dyscalculia as: difficulty in judging the number of items in an array without counting them (subitising), even when the set is very small; difficulty in judging the reasonableness of answers involving numbers; memory weaknesses; inability to count backwards correctly. She includes visual and spatial orientation weaknesses, along with difficulty identifying left and right directions, difficulties with sequences and patterns, and slow speed of processing in arithmetical/mathematical tasks. Difficulties also apply in wider number-related tasks, so that money identification and calculation, time-telling and time management are also problematic (Bird, 2013: 5).

Steve Chinn's (2012) checklist offers 31 characteristics, providing additional detail. Characteristics of dyscalculia with particular relevance to young children include:

*   finding it impossible to see that (e.g.) four objects are four, without counting (or three objects, if a young child);
*   counting all the numbers when adding, e.g. five plus three, counts 12345 ... 678;
*   finding it difficult to count fluently sequences that are less familiar, e.g. one, three, five, seven ...;
*   having difficulty in progressing from apparatus and images to direct calculation;
*   organising written work poorly, e.g. without lining up numbers properly;
*   failing to recognise automatically that (e.g.) seven plus five is the same as five plus seven;
*   writing 51 for 15 or 61 for 16 (and the same reversal for all the teen numbers);
*   struggling with mental arithmetic;
*   getting very anxious about doing any mathematics tasks, refusing to attempt them, particularly when they are unfamiliar, or hurrying the work;
*   being unable to 'see' patterns or sequences, especially unfamiliar ones (ibid.: 17–27).

As in literacy, these characteristics bear a relationship to the performance of younger children, so practitioners will need to decide whether a child's difficulty falls within a regular range of expectation, or whether it is time to offer interventions. In this case the interventions are concerned with secure counting, secure judgement of magnitude and being able to recognise the number of items making up small sets. The same range of small-step, multisensory approaches that apply to literacy, revised and revisited, will need to be applied to number work. The first step will be to make sure that finger-counting is established.

The relationship between maths and science

Mathematics is considered to be the tool of science, providing the means by which science explores and records phenomena in the world. Given the difficulties in literacy and perhaps also in arithmetical/mathematical calculation that can occur with dyslexia, it might seem that science is particularly problematic. However, this is not necessarily the case. Science explores the real world, and since the real world is full of interest for young children, natural curiosity can be encouraged in the development of science-based activity.

Dyslexia disguises the levels of ability among learners because of the requirement that input and output take place through literacy. While basic arithmetic may cause difficulties for some learners, adult testimonials point to the fact that higher order mathematics skills may nevertheless be accessible. Difficulties with arithmetic may not always indicate mathematical problems across the whole field. Conceptual leaps leading to mathematical insights may not be encouraged when learners are acquiring arithmetical skills, but there is a higher level of mathematical endeavour beyond arithmetic, where a more abstract conceptualisation is required. Just as some dyslexic people can be particularly adept at creative or practical activities, some may be especially skilled in higher-order mathematics, or the sciences.

Dyslexia-aware practitioners will not rule out children's potential because they are struggling with particular aspects of learning. Instead, they can make use of dyslexia-friendly methods including the use of diagrams, plans, charts, graphic representations and recording methods that do not rely on writing. The practical nature of scientific study can be an asset to dyslexic learners.

Because of the relationship between mathematics and science, their vocabulary is closely linked and insights about mathematics vocabulary are pertinent. Abel and Exley (2008), in researching mathematical assessments in early education, found that the mathematical vocabulary used may exceed considerably the level of literacy expected of that age range, creating barriers for potential or actual dyslexic learners. Furthermore, dyslexia may cause arithmetical/mathematical or scientific concepts to be mapped incorrectly onto mathematical or scientific actions because there are mistakes in reading the written terms. Even when this is not the case, vocabulary may not be taught in dyslexia-aware ways, may not be learnt, or understood, or retained, or accessed.

Responsive teaching for numeracy

Most children gain necessary number skills. Where this does not happen, ever-increasing attempts to explain, from a position of knowledge, may not help. A responsive teaching approach involves thinking about what we are doing in our pedagogical interactions and trying to improve them. Even if there is no apparent interference from literacy demands, practices need to be in place to help learners who are struggling with number concepts. A practitioner needs to be willing and able to:

1. use apparatus and demonstration for as long as necessary;
2. explore a child's arithmetical/mathematical thinking, rolling it backwards step by step until they find a place where knowledge is both accurate and secure, before guiding it forward along correct pathways;
3. use very small steps in putting correct knowledge into place. This requires both patience and the ability to analyse an arithmetical task, not just to impart it;
4. find the time and opportunity to do this as and when needed;
5. pay particular attention to ensuring that arithmetical vocabulary is appropriate, clearly understood and correctly and consistently used by all.

Goouch and Lambrith (2011) point out that teachers learn from children while children learn from teachers; learning is collaborative and responsive. It is the role of adults to provide guidance, and a model of competence, but a responsive approach expects that children will share and join in with the learning endeavour. In considering reading, the authors emphasise the importance of both adults and children talking about texts, sharing enthusiasm about them and exploring them. In this way, children become attuned to a culture of reading, and are able to continue with enthusiasm and exploration themselves. A similarly language-based approach could help young children to learn about number concepts, with practitioners 'discussing' with learners rather than 'telling' them. As the authors point out, 'Learning depends on the negotiation of meaning' (ibid.: 118). While numbers and arithmetical concepts themselves may be seen as fixed, in the same way as an alphabet, meanings are not necessarily obvious; they develop by being shared and shaped through discussion and through adult guidance.

Dyslexia-aware principles: numeracy 'catch-up' strategies

The Department for Education in England (DfE, 2012) describes 'catch-up' strategies for both literacy and numeracy. While children who experience dyslexia or dyscalculia are likely to find it difficult to catch up before their peers have moved on, the principles are of value in teaching and learning for all children. Citing Slavin *et al.* (2009), the document notes that 'the most successful mathematics programmes focused on changing daily teaching practices, particularly the use of cooperative learning methods, classroom management, and motivation programmes. The most successful mathematics programmes encouraged pupil interaction' (DfE, 2012: 5). These principles are all pertinent to the learning needs of children who experience dyslexia and/or dyscalculia.

For primary children who are 'low attainers' in mathematics, the document suggests strategies that are familiar to dyslexia-aware teachers. These include noticing early when children are having difficulties, putting in place interventions to help them, perhaps on a one-to-one basis, and monitoring and assessing these carefully. It also recommends training practitioners in approaches such as cooperative/collaborative learning. Early support to overcome difficulties is felt to counteract the development of mathematics fear, in home-school and peer-to-peer work as well as in classroom work.

The document encourages the development of cognitive approaches. As discussed, these include mapping of items onto fingers in early counting, then set enumeration and recognition of the relative size of sets. To these may be added the recognition of numbers as symbols and words, and memory, retrieval and 'attentional control' for number facts and processes (Hulme and Snowling, 2009: 184).

Dyslexia-aware practice: multiplication tables

At around the ages of six to eight years, children in schools start to learn their multiplication tables, although some may start earlier and some may not master them until later. Meehan (2013) advocates the display of multiplication tables in a classroom; Bacon and Handley's (2014) findings about the importance of visual learning strategies can make them more dyslexia-friendly. Appendix 5 shows a dyslexia-aware layout for a multiplication table which adapts the ranks of numbers so that they are no longer a solid block, difficult to discern. While classroom walls may have conventional display charts for tables, smaller sheets with layouts such as these can be offered for individual work. The sheet can be used for linking numbers with arrows or identifying patterns, and can be otherwise drawn on or decorated, to reduce the fear factor.

Information and communication technology: computing, coding and programmable toys

Computing, or computer science, is a recent focus within early curricula in many countries. This moves computer use beyond play, information-gathering and recording activities, towards programming and designing programs. Computing activities address the ways in which children will be connected to their world, including the ways in which they solve problems and carry out tasks. In this respect, they are part of the lifelong learning agenda, where the development of early skills is seen as important for later opportunities supporting growth and development. There can be little doubt of the importance of computers in children's futures.

Subject content for computing in the UK National Curriculum includes not only effective use of computers for a range of purposes, but also understanding on a level that enables young learners to predict, evaluate, create, organise and rectify content. This understanding is expected to encompass the wider range of information technology devices encountered in daily use. In particular, children now learn to write programs themselves, through coding. In this way, learners are transformed, at their own level, from passive consumers to active developers of ICT.

The writing of code in order to program a computer involves making a sequence of small-step instructions written in the particular language or style of coding (an algorithm). These have to be sequenced correctly for the desired computer operation to be successful. Errors have to be found and corrected (debugging), otherwise the desired operation or action will not take place. Instructional programs provide young children with the experience of making and amending instructions through coding; useful, explanatory activities of this kind can be explored through websites such as BBC KS1 Computer Science (http://www.bbc.co.uk/) and Barclays Code Playground (http://www.barclays.co.uk/).

For very young children, programming begins with remote-controlled toys, their activities controlled by a joystick or a mouse. Children advance to resources such as Beebot®, where a sequence can be programmed into the toy and stored, in order to make the toy move from one place to another. With activities of this kind the signs, symbols and language associated with computer programming begin to be applied. Children are not required to interpret writing in order to carry out activities or solve problems; the practical outcomes of their coding of the robot can be seen immediately. Digital Blue (http://www.digitalblue.org.uk/) provides cards with which the stages of a sequence can be planned out before being programmed into the robot.

As with the introduction of phonics, this is a new emphasis in modern curricula and it remains to be seen how it will affect learners with actual or possible dyslexia. While sequencing is one of the areas that dyslexic learners often find difficult, the nature of coding is that it involves few words, letters, or numbers and, when used, these are within clear boundaries. The sequence requirements are clear, being laid out like a flow chart; the impact of an incorrect sequence is immediately apparent and the need to correct it is instant. There remains a need for word, letter or number identification, but this information is required in small packets, increasing the chances of accuracy.

The impact of dyslexia has to be accommodated, whether its effect in computing is upon words, letters, or numbers. Dr Mike James, editor of the website I Programmer (http://www.i-programmer.info/), notes that there are many highly skilled program-mers who are also dyslexic. They may have their own particular characteristics which, once recognised, can be watched for – by the programmers themselves and their co-workers. What is noteworthy is that dyslexic programmers have explored the opportu-nity to go beyond the basic requirements of arithmetic into a mathematical area where other skills and characteristics can come into play. Enabling this to happen remains a challenge for practitioners. While the early focus is likely to be upon arithmetic, never-theless, computing and coding may open new mathematical avenues for young learners with potential or actual dyslexia.

Learning game: decoding the letter/picture/number code

Pictures and letters: a class can suggest ideas for supplying simple drawings to match letter sounds; this may need to be done over several sessions and a practitioner needs to be willing to draw the pictures! The code is put on paper or card for table use and/or on a wall chart for class use. Three-letter words in the form of the drawings are prepared on cards and, working in pairs, groups or tables, children are challenged to decode them and blend them into words. With experience, children may try encoding simple words themselves.

Numbers and letters: a code is displayed by assigning a number to each letter; then children decode the letters via the numbers, blending them to give simple three-letter words. Children may try encoding words themselves and pass around the numbers for decoding.

Adapted from McNicholas and McEntee (1991, 2004), no. 51: Phonic Discrimination – Pictographs (p. 35) and no. 57: Reading for Meaning – Number Codes (p. 44).

How can dyslexia be supported in these games?

- Dyslexic learners often report the value of attaching a visual cue to a letter/sound; where children have nominated the pictures themselves, the value of the cue is stronger.
- Dyslexic learners often have difficulty transferring information from a board to their work, so a wall chart on its own is not enough – table copies are needed.
- The number of letters in the main code can be reduced to be more manageable. A practitioner does not have to tackle the whole alphabet at once; for example, letter sounds can reflect preferred phonics sequences.
- Working in pairs or groups will support a potentially dyslexic learner by helping them to learn from peers, reducing possible tension in adult-to-pupil transactions.
- If children go on to encode words for themselves, a child who is creative or skilled at drawing can shine. Even if they do not generate three-letter words themselves, potentially dyslexic children can hear and take notice when words are generated by others.

- Number code strings can be decorated with picture clues.
- Practitioners can watch to see whether a child who has difficulty with sounds and letters also has difficulty with drawing, or with numbers strings.

Attitude, understanding, technique, empathy: building mathematics and science skills

There is considerable interest in improving arithmetical/mathematical accessibility and performance. Practitioners can support arithmetical/mathematical learning for young children through:

- *attitude*: believing that children can succeed in number work if the right way is found to teach them because of the innate sense of number experienced by even very young children;
- *understanding*: realising that correcting errors does not help a child improve their mathematics skills – they need to work through the correct process with a practitioner;
- *technique*: being aware of the need to use supportive multisensory apparatus and activities to create a foundation for literacy and numeracy, carried on for longer;
- *empathy*: appreciating the nature of mathematics anxiety and the need to guide children forward with small, patient steps in order to overcome this.

Recommended reading

1. Department for Education (2012) *Literacy and Numeracy Catch-up Strategies*, London, DfE
2. Bird, R. (2013) *The Dyscalculia Toolkit* (2nd edn), London, SAGE
3. Chinn, S. (2012) *More Trouble with Maths*, Abingdon, NASEN/Routledge

Useful websites

1. http://map.mathshell.org
   This website describes the Maths Assessment Project, which constitutes part of the Bill and Melinda Gates Foundation Maths Design Collaborative. This involves joint working between the Shell Centre for Mathematical Education, the University of California at Berkeley and the University of Nottingham. Although the content is aimed at older children, the Classroom Challenges lesson structure is of relevance for younger ones, helping them to develop into powerful mathematical thinkers. The embedded publication, A Brief Guide for Teachers and Administrators, includes design principles and features for mathematical teaching and learning.
2. http://www.ronitbird.com/
   Ronit Bird's website includes the embedded publication Top Ten Tips for Parents of Dyscalculic Children, details about her publications and courses and free resources for the UK National Curriculum.
3. http://www.coreknowledge.org.uk/
   This is the website for Core Knowledge UK, a project which is run by Civitas, an educational charity and provider. It provides free resources and activities for the UK National Curriculum for use at home and at school.

MY DYSLEXIA EXPERIENCE: PROGRAMMING

One odd symptom that is very rarely discussed, but a number of dyslexics I have known recognise it when it is mentioned, is a strange symmetric transposition of whole character or figure groups.

For example, one person I work with always confuses the numbers 12 and 20 to the point where if I find a 12 or a 20 in a program there is a 50% probability it should have been the other one!

Why 12 and why 20?

A good question, but you can see, or rather hear, that there is similarity in the way that they sound – yes the problems are complicated and sometimes comical!

(Dr Mike James, 2014, Dyslexia and Programming, I PROGRAMMER,
http://www.i-programmer.info/)

References

Abel, K. and Exley, B. (2008) Using Halliday's Functional Grammar to Examine Early Years Worded Mathematics Texts, *Australian Journal of Language and Literacy*, 31, 3, 227–41

Bacon, A. and Handley, S. (2014) Reasoning and Dyslexia: Is Visual Memory a Compensatory Resource?, *Dyslexia*, 20, 4, 330–45

Bird, R. (2013) *The Dyscalculia Toolkit* (2nd edn), London, SAGE

Butterworth, B., Varma, S. and Laurillard, D. (2011) Dyscalculia: From Brain to Education, *Science*, 332, 1049–53

Chinn, S. (2012) *More Trouble With Maths*, Abingdon, NASEN/Routledge

Department for Education (2012) *Literacy and Numeracy Catch-up Strategies*, London, DfE

Evans, T., Flowers, D., Napoliello, E., Olulade, O. and Eden, G. (2014) The Functional Anatomy of Single-digit Arithmetic in Children with Developmental Dyslexia, *Neuroimage*, 101, 644–52

Goouch, K. and Lambrith, A. (2011) *Teaching Early Reading and Phonics*, London, SAGE

Hulme, C. and Snowling, M. (2009) *Developmental Disorders of Language Learning and Cognition*, Malden, Wiley-Blackwell

James, M. (2014) Dyslexia and Programming, *I PROGRAMMER*, available online at: http//www.i-programmer.info/

Marino, C., Mascheretti, S., Riva, V., Cattaneo, F., Rigoletto, C., Rusconi, M., Gruen, J., Giorda, R., Lazazzera, C. and Molteni, M. (2011) Pleiotropic Effects of DCDC2 and DYX1C1 Genes on Language and Mathematics Traits in Nuclear Families of Developmental Dyslexia, *Behaviour Genetics*, 41, 1, 67–76

McNicholas, J. and McEntee, J. (1991, 2004) *Games to Improve Reading Levels*, NASEN/Routledge

Meehan, M. (2013) Dyslexia and Mathematics, in B. Pavey, M. Meehan and S. Davis, *The Dyslexia-Friendly Teacher's Toolkit*, London, SAGE

Slavin, R., Lake, C. and Groff, C. (2009) *What Works in Teaching Maths? Report Summary*, York, Institute for Effective Education, University of York

Szűchs, D. and Goswami, U. (2013) Developmental Dyscalculia: Fresh Perspectives (Editorial), *Trends in Neuroscience and Education*, 2, 2, 33–7

Vukovic, R., Kieffer, M., Bailey, S. and Harari, R. (2013) Mathematics Anxiety in Young Children: Concurrent and Longitudinal Associations with Mathematical Performance, *Contemporary Educational Psychology*, 38, 1, 1–10

Chapter 10

Play and creativity in the support for dyslexia

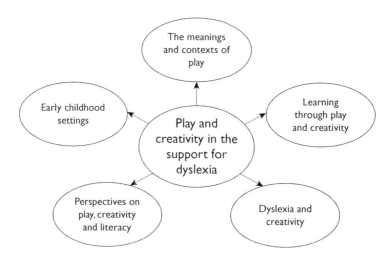

Good practice points

For good practice we need to:

1. provide opportunities for play for its own sake, as well as for pedagogic purposes;
3. use playfulness and good humour to lighten the learning load;
4. provide opportunities for divergent thinking in young children;
4. encourage active listening;
5. provide a range of materials and resources for creative work, including good-quality materials, but also found and repurposed ones.

The meanings and contexts of play

There are diverse viewpoints about what constitutes play and how, or indeed whether, it should be supported by adults; these may be found in different settings for young children. Tina Bruce (2015: 2) identifies three typical ways of viewing young children; they can be seen as 'blank sheets', needing an adult's influence and guidance (an 'empiricist' approach); or as natural beings who need to be allowed to unfold, themselves, according to nature (a 'nativist' view), or as a combination of the two (an 'interactivist' view). Bruce relates these back to seventeenth-century philosophical views, but still finds them evident today, influencing the way that play is viewed and made available.

The role of adults in play is linked to the play philosophy. In a time of increasing emphasis upon early literacy and numeracy, teachers still consider that free-choice playing, especially when it involves pretend play, is crucial for young children's psycho-social development (Berkhout *et al.*, 2010). Play offers opportunities for children to be creative, to use toys and materials creatively and to develop explanations and narratives of their own, although these may be mediated by adults.

In present-day education systems, play – and learning through play – is generally assigned to the experience of very young children. There are different ways of enabling play, according to the adult policies or beliefs involved. It may be 'free', where children follow their own instincts and preferences, or it may be part of a structured curriculum. It may include the principle of 'free-flow' play (Bruce, 2015), utilising indoor and outdoor play areas. Bruce states that 'Play is an integrating mechanism that allows flexible, adaptive, imaginative, innovative behaviour. Play makes children into whole people, able to keep balancing their lives in a fast-changing world so that they are both "grounded" and together' (ibid.: 73). However, Grieshaber and McArdle (2010) challenge some of the beliefs about children's play, pointing out that it can also be a means of maintaining status or asserting power, with social and 'political' aspects that do not always result in pleasantness and fun.

Robson and Rowe (2012) show that while exploratory play of all kinds helps children to develop creative thinking, it is outdoor play, including gardening and construction, and 'socio-dramatic' play which are noticeably valuable. In such play and creative activity young children with possible or actual dyslexia can build their knowledge and explore their individual skills, abilities and talents, regardless of any measured intelligence or ability levels. Socio-dramatic activity, in particular, is seen by Robson and Rowe as facilitating creative thinking.

Learning through play and creativity

The use of play to help young children to learn seems like a natural progression in children's early education, so play is a cross-agency concern. Multi-agency health, care and education teams use play to encourage the growth of physical, cognitive and communication abilities in young children who are identified, usually soon after their birth, as being in need of developmental support. Team members work in homes with parents and caregivers, advising about toys and activities and supporting the transition to preschool provision. Play and creative activity can also provide a valuable means of expression and communication between social workers and young children in receipt of social care. From earliest stages, play is used to boost physical, cognitive and emotional development.

Bodrova and Leong (2010: 3) use the term 'playful learning' to describe adult-led activities that use elements of play or fun in learning. In order to help dyslexic children to gain necessary skills and to remain buoyant in the face of difficulty, good practice recommends the use of a range of multisensory and creative activities; these can also include humour and fun. This has relevance for dyslexia, so long as it does not include teasing; schooling is already a sensitive matter for some children. However, Saifer (2010) questions whether children themselves see such activities as play-like, since they are adult led. For this reason, and to reassure parents and caregivers, it is perhaps important to present such activities as another way of learning, rather than play in the sense of work's opposite. For dyslexic learners such techniques may make the difference between learning being lost or being retained and applied.

Learning games and, more recently, 'serious games' have been developed across a broad range of education and training settings, offering simulation and rehearsal to facilitate learning through electronic means. Gaggi *et al.* (2012) employ the concept of 'serious games' to describe computer activities designed by them to both identify young learners at risk of dyslexia and to train them in the precursor skills of visual and auditory discrimination, and the focusing of attention/avoidance of distraction when presented with stimuli. Gaggi *et al.* point out that a game-like task increases children's enjoyment and engagement in activities, and subsequently increases the amount of skills practice that they undertake. By using serious games and playful learning, practitioners and caregivers can ease the transition to literacy activity for children with potential or actual dyslexia, without undermining their confidence.

Dyslexia and creativity

Possible links between dyslexia and creativity have been of interest for some time. In the 1960s Guilford developed the concept of divergent thinking; this is still considered to be a characteristic of creative activity, while creativity is, itself, considered by some to be a characteristic of dyslexia. Indeed, some authors (see, for example, Eide and Eide, 2010) consider that it is a mistake to focus upon aspects and skills that dyslexic individuals cannot accomplish easily; it would be more helpful to focus on their positive characteristics and to see dyslexia as an inadvertent consequence of other, more useful traits. Creativity in dyslexic individuals is often linked to a person's abilities to think differently, to see things differently and to reach novel solutions and conclusions.

The tendencies among some dyslexic individuals to see the 'big picture', to make conceptual leaps (often seen as creative actions), to notice and focus upon different aspects of a situation and to follow a different pathway rather than an expected 'logical', linear sequence, are all part of the testimonial evidence of dyslexic people. These characteristics can contribute fresh ideas, new perspectives, innovation and entrepreneurship to a range of processes and contexts. They can be valued for extending the boundaries of thought and practice.

The concept of whether creativity is itself a dyslexic characteristic has been contested. While some studies suggest that there might be more people with dyslexia than expected in creative activities, this does not necessarily mean that there is a causal link. Where someone's cognitive profile is constrained by dyslexia it would not be surprising to find increased development, described by some as compensatory, in other areas; the question has been whether or not this is an innate capability.

A number of recent studies have indicated that there seems to be no causal link between dyslexia and creativity. Ritchie *et al.* (2013) found higher reading scores associated with higher creativity scores; Alves and Nakano (2014) found higher creativity linked to higher intelligence, with no significant difference between the dyslexic and non-dyslexic groups in their research; Mourgues, Preiss and Grigorenko (2014) found that higher verbal ability was linked to higher creativity and insight. For the present, at least, it seems that where creativity is significant, its link is with measures of intelligence rather than with dyslexia.

Perspectives on play, creativity and literacy

Grieshaber and McArdle (2010) feel that play and creative activity have become somewhat synonymous. It is certainly the case that children's use of creative media is generally presented as one of a number of available choices for play and in this play children are learning to master creative methods and materials. When 'creativity' takes this form, Grieshaber and McArdle (ibid.) consider that taking part in an art activity has become an end in itself. They see painting and modelling as activities which young children are set to carry out without the activities leading anywhere, being linked to anything, or being carried through into further development.

Creative activities can be taken further, however, with teaching and learning built around them. After World War II Sybil Marshall (1963) developed the idea of teaching through the arts, using this experience not just to teach art, but also to support all her teaching. Working with mixed infant and junior classes, Marshall taught her pupils conventionally but she also gave her pupils opportunities for creative experience and expression, in both the visual and the performing arts. She encouraged them to develop individual pieces and also whole-class, long-term projects that engaged their enthusiasm and commitment. Within this process children made aesthetic judgements about how they employed their materials, and about the aesthetic power of their own, and others', finished artwork. Marshall's work showed that creativity could be carried out for its own sake and for the benefit of other learning.

Early childhood settings

Early years education is now global. There is generally a range of state and private provision available and while there may be differences, there are also common characteristics. These include the promotion of children's growth and development and an interest in the development of cognition, of social behaviour, of creativity, of play and of relationships. They may or may not include a concern with the direct acquisition of literacy skills, but all are aware of the importance of language development. The range of early childhood settings available internationally includes some which have gained support because of the philosophies and styles of education that they offer. Three such examples are: Reggio Emilia schools; Steiner Waldorf schools; and Montessori schools.

Reggio Emilia schools: There are social as well as creative aspects to the Reggio Emilia perspective, which was a post-war initiative that, over time, has gained worldwide respect among educators of young children. Loris Malaguzzi, the founder, espoused children's rights and saw children's development as progressing via relationships in a social context that involved everyone; his was a positive view:

> Children have the right to imagine. We need to give them full rights of citizenship in life and in society. It's necessary that we believe that the child is very intelligent, that the child is strong and beautiful and has very ambitious desires and requests. This is the image of the child that we need to hold.
>
> (Malaguzzi, 1994: 5)

In this setting children's play is seen as a source that enables adults to observe and learn about how children think, act and interact, and the recording of such observations is a practice that is now widespread in early years education.

A considerable value is placed upon the arts in the Reggio Emilia approach. Reggio Emilia schools offer preschool provision, so that the direct teaching of literacy is not likely to be seen as a factor. However, language and literacy development is an important part of the teaching and learning. The phrase 'the hundred languages of children' is used by Malaguzzi to describe the many ways that children find to express themselves, their ideas and their learning, and these are encouraged through the value given to creative activity. Schools have a creative space called an 'atelier', with an 'atelierista', who is a practitioner with an arts or other creative professional background, and who works with the children.

Steiner Waldorf schools: Another setting that promotes creativity is that originating in the work and philosophy of Rudolf Steiner. This particular philosophy has generated some controversy, but, in terms of teaching and learning, there is a considerable value placed upon play and creative activity (Woods *et al.*, 2005). The Steiner Waldorf approach does not include formal teaching of literacy skills until children enter the appropriate class, described as being at 'six plus' years of age (Steiner Waldorf Education, 2011: 22), but in other respects there is a relationship with early years objectives.

Emergent literacy skills form part of this learning environment, in the form of language development, word recognition of a more spontaneous kind, mark-making and the use of pretend reading and writing within play. Imagination, creativity, aesthetic appreciation and ability in the arts, crafts and music are all important within the Steiner Waldorf approach: 'Imaginary play is considered the most important "work" of the young child and the activity through which the child grows physically, intellectually, and emotionally' (Edwards, 2002).

Montessori schools: While play activity is present in the practical activities that children undertake in this setting, the approach developed from the work of Maria Montessori does not encourage imaginary play of the role-playing kind until children are older.

Another particular feature is that early literacy skills using multisensory learning are part of the Montessori curriculum from a young age. Children experience a wide range of foundational activities which encourage their interest in words, books and print, and which help them to develop the requisite skills they will need for more formal literacy learning. This leads, in turn, to developments in phonological awareness and the reading and writing of simple, then more complex, words (Isaacs, 2015).

Considering the Reggio Emilia, Steiner Waldorf and Montessori approaches together, Edwards confirms that the models all have a basis in wanting to make a better social and pedagogic experience for children. She points out that these perspectives vary in the roles of professionals in relation to children, their interactions, the learning experiences they provide and the ways in which they observe and record children's development (Edwards, 2002). Nevertheless, many of the ideas originating with these models have had a sustained influence which can be found throughout modern early years practice today.

A relatively recent approach, HighScope, was developed in the 1960s by David Weikart and his colleagues. Like others, this has a social purpose in seeking to improve the lives and opportunities of disadvantaged children. HighScope follows a curriculum and a structure for activities, but also allows for children's choices. It supports 'active learning through play', with teachers supporting and encouraging the extension of children's thinking and problem-solving. The curriculum includes, currently, 58 key development indicators (KDIs), which are broad descriptors linked to developmental progression. The list of KDIs covers a wide range, including aspects concerned with play, creative activity and language and literacy development.

Planning is important in the HighScope strategy, and the 'plan–do–review' process is an important part of its pedagogy. Children plan what they are going to do in 'small group time', then they carry out their planned activity – they can change their mind if they wish – and review it in a plenary-type 'large group time'. From these outcomes adults plan activities for the next day (Marshall, 2013). For children with potential or actual dyslexia this type of planning process might well be advantageous. It could help in creating an understanding of step-wise sequences and the efforts involved in following through the planned activities.

Dyslexia-aware principles: playfulness

Jones and Reynolds (2015) describe the range of ways in which teachers become involved in play; they might facilitate, record, plan or mediate play, or sometimes interrupt or divert it. Practitioners are used to seeing play as a means to an end, and as discussed, the inclusion of playfulness and humour may lighten spirits, increasing interest and building confidence for children who may find literacy and numeracy particularly difficult. Play is a valuable way of developing vocabulary and grammar, and research suggests that children who learn playfully also learn well (Harris et al. 2011). However for some adults playfulness is problematic. It may be difficult for a practitioner to approach learning playfully when they are beset by pressures and targets that increase anxiety, and pedagogical demands that take up any available time. Free play may be viewed as 'downtime' for both children and practitioners; it might be valued for that function, or in contrast, seen as time which detracts from study.

For children who experience potential or actual dyslexia, play is doubly important as the time when they are not under pressure from the pedagogical areas that they find most difficult. When practitioners want to know more about how to help a child who is experiencing language, literacy or numeracy difficulties, information may be gained by playing with that child. The play would be a child's choice, and on principle a practitioner would ensure it was free, responsive, and without pedagogical loading. If play calls on the play activities associated with a younger child, a practitioner need not be concerned or make assumptions about a child, but be open to learning about them, from them.

Dyslexia-aware practice: active listening

Active listening is an idea that comes from communication and life skills, describing how we show that we are listening. Active listening techniques include body language and eye contact, sympathetic expressions, gestures and head movements, encouraging sounds and comments like 'mmm-hmm', 'go on', etc.; all these help to keep communication flowing. We may not find these in young children. Nevertheless, we need small children to attend to us and, for some, this may be a new idea that needs practice. We can explain that concentrating means that 'all' their eyes, their ears and their attention is upon us. We can make eye contact, to make sure of children's attention. We can seek active listening in a number of ways – stopping what we are saying in order to elicit responses from children, or asking for a show of hands, or a particular gesture.

A common method of ensuring active listening is to omit words from songs, stories, or sentences and to expect children to supply them. However, it is not helpful to take children by surprise with a question, even though this is probably a traditional approach. 'Spot' quizzes are not kind to children who experience potential or actual dyslexia; an unexpected question scatters concentration, possibly inducing fear, and a dyslexic child may not be able to retrieve the words they want. It would be more useful to invoke active listening by suggesting that children ask us a question about what they have seen and heard within a topic, making sure that they know this is going to happen.

Information and communication technology: *Sesame Street*, *Nick Jr* and *CBeebies*

Television channels have included programmes specifically for children almost since their beginning and, over time, they have developed educational functions alongside their entertainment role, to the extent that educational content may now be a required part of a company's remit. Educational programming has kept pace with modern technology and, whereas there are many apps and games intended to support young children's learning, those developed by companies with longstanding experience of children's broadcasting have valued credentials. All three providers discussed here make significant use of play and creativity.

Sesame Street has an international audience and its character and format are very familiar. Starting in the 1960s, its objectives were social as well as educational; its remit was always to educate through good-quality children's television. *Sesame Street*'s target audience was disadvantaged, at-risk, preschool children; the programmes aimed to help them to get ready for school. The programme-makers created a curriculum consisting of cognitive and affective areas. They drew on research to develop programmes consisting of small segments and including literacy and early mathematics components, health and wellbeing. Diversity was a strong characteristic of the scenes and stories; the programmes included, as standard, different cultures, nationalities and languages. Humour and music remain significant features of *Sesame Street*'s approach. Today, the familiar teaching and learning formats are available through the *Sesame Street* website, linked to the well-known Muppet characters (http://www.sesamestreet.org/).

Nickelodeon, from Canada, was launched at the end of the 1970s, seeking to follow the *Sesame Street* approach. Programmes are provided for a younger, preschool audience through its channel Nick Jr. Unlike the other two providers, Nickelodeon and Nick Jr include advertising. However, the programme-makers are keen to use advertisements responsibly and to carry out research on the impact of children's use of media and responses to advertising (http://www.nickjr.co.uk/).

CBeebies is made by the UK public broadcasting company BBC and is an offshoot of its children's programming. Launched in 2002, the website features shows, games, music, activities for joining in and creative activities; the content connects with BBC children's television and radio (http://www.bbc.co.uk/cbeebies).

All three companies carry a range of games, videos (with links to TV programmes) and well-known cartoon characters. There are sections for creative activities and alphabet and number activities and there is information for parents attached to each segment. *Sesame Street* and Nick Jr present some features in the Spanish language. All three have guidance for parents included in their websites and all three have free apps available for the 'i' Operating System and Android.

Learning game: make a snake – supporting left–right orientation and word recognition

This game supports left–right orientation of word writing and sequencing, word finding, rhyming, word beginnings and endings, letter combinations, etc. A practitioner supplies a paper with a snake drawn on it, divided into segments which are left blank. The snake drawing has some elements of decoration for colouring in. The number of segments would depend on how many words a practitioner wanted children to find, perhaps starting with three. On the tail the practitioner places the starting stimulus; it could be a sound/letter, or it could be a word. Children work in pairs or groups; the 'snake' task can be carried out in a number of ways:

a)   A stimulus sound/letter is placed on the tail. Children have to find words that start with that sound/letter, providing one word for each segment.

b) A stimulus word is placed on the tail. Children have to find a word that starts with the end sound/letter of that word. They do the same with the next segments, looking for a word that starts with the end sound/letter of the last one, in a domino effect, until all segments are finished.

c) A stimulus word is placed on the tail. Children have to find rhyming words. A practitioner would need to decide for him or herself how they are going to treat words that sound the same but are spelt differently. Lists of words in English often come up against alternative spellings, so a practitioner must make it clear, from the start, what is being sought in this activity.

d) A stimulus letter combination, e.g. phonic blend or digraph, is placed on the tail. Children have to find words that use that combination – in the middle, or the beginning, or the end, according to requirements.

The snakes are decorated, displayed and used in teaching and learning. A further creative element can be introduced by using the results to make a giant game of snakes and ladders, or a jungle picture. A practitioner can confirm this purpose to children at the start of the activity: 'We are going to make (- - -) but first we need some snakes … these are going to be word snakes!'

Adapted from McNicholas and McEntee (1991, 2004), no. 65: Rhyming Snake – Reading and Writing Word Game (p. 48).

How can dyslexia be supported in these games?

* Some dyslexic learners may have difficulties with following sequences or linear logic. The snake format provides a frame and training for these elements.
* Practitioners often group together children when they have difficulties; this is an understandable strategy that is based on the idea that it gives opportunities for more intense working with that group. However, the recommended dyslexia practice is that children with potential or actual dyslexia should be educated at their ability level rather than their literacy level. It would be preferable to give preparatory input separately, so that, when it comes to the game, children could join in with their peers.
* A dyslexia-aware practitioner would want to be very clear about the teaching point they are making with their chosen task. It is possible to become diverted by an alternative spelling and to be sidetracked into giving explanatory input at that time. It would be preferable, to avoid confusion for children with potential or actual dyslexia, to note that some spellings of a particular sound are not always the same and to focus input on that point at another time.

Attitude, understanding, technique, empathy: play and creativity

We can allow playfulness and creativity into our interactions with young children, while maintaining a responsible stance through:

* *attitude*: generally keeping our mood light and encouraging for children, while reserving the right to be serious sometimes;

- *understanding*: knowing that divergent thinking is not 'wrong' thinking and can be exciting and useful, but that it is important to return focus to the matter in hand, when necessary;
- *technique*: inviting children to ask us questions and sometimes prompting them to allow thinking to 'take flight', exploring creative, imaginative, higher-order thinking;
- *empathy*: being aware that play can be used by some children in power relationships over others, in ways that hurt them.

Recommended reading

1. Bruce, T. (2015) *Early Childhood Education* (5th edn), Abingdon, Hodder Education
2. Edwards, C. (2002) Three Approaches from Europe: Waldorf, Montessori, and Reggio Emilia, *Early Childhood Research and Practice: An Internet Journal on the Development, Care, and Education of Young Children*, 4, 1, 1–14
3. MacKay, N. (2012) *Removing Dyslexia as a Barrier to Achievement* (3rd edn), Wakefield, SEN Marketing

Useful websites

1. http://www.arvindguptatoys.com/
   Arvind Gupta invents toys from local and discarded materials and uses them to connect play to mathematics and science. He has won many awards for his work; his Technology, Entertainment and Design (TED) talk Turning Trash Into Toys (available via the website and YouTube) is considered one of the best. The website hosts a text-only version of Sybil Marshall's book *An Experiment in Education*, at http://www.arvindguptatoys.com/arvindgupta/sybil.pdf
2. http://www.reggiochildren.it/
   This is an official website for the Reggio Emilia approach. It contains details of the international movement that Reggio Emilia has become, with information about the approach and related events, publications and research.
3. www.silkysteps.com/
   Silkysteps is a website for preschool play and creative activities, originating with, and managed by, Ruth Grimes. It contains a wealth of ideas, suggestions for activities and free, printable resources; its discussion forums are much appreciated by parents and caregivers. The activities have useful links to early years sector skills.

MY DYSLEXIA EXPERIENCE: OUR CREATIVE CHILD

My daughter's creative abilities shone through before she started school. She would draw and paint, sing and dance, pretend to be other people. At that time, we, as her parents, had no knowledge of the literacy difficulties that lay ahead. How I wish we could have spared her. We were lucky that someone recognised her potential and she was able to specialise in dance and drama. She has a career now. She is still dyslexic, but she gets round it. (Parent)

References

Alves, R. and Nakano, T. (2014) Creativity and Intelligence in Children With and Without Developmental Dyslexia, *Paidéia (Ribeirão Preto)* [online], 24, 59, 361–9

Berkhout, L., Dolk, M. and Goorhuis-Brouwer, S. (2010) Teachers' Views on Psychosocial Development in Children from 4 to 6 Years of Age, *Educational and Child Psychology*, 27, 4, 103–12

Bodrova, E. and Leong, D. (2010) Curriculum and Play in Early Child Development, in R. Tremblay, M. Boivin and R. Peters (eds), *Encyclopedia on Early Childhood Development*, Montreal, Quebec: Centre of Excellence for Early Childhood Development and Strategic Knowledge Cluster on Early Child Development: 1–6, available at: http://www.child-encyclopedia.com/

Bruce, T. (2015) *Early Childhood Education* (5th edn), Abingdon, Hodder Education

Edwards, C. (2002) Three Approaches from Europe: Waldorf, Montessori, and Reggio Emilia, *Early Childhood Research and Practice: An Internet Journal on the Development, Care, and Education of Young Children*, 4, 1, 1–14

Eide, B. and Eide, F. (2010) *The Dyslexic Advantage*, London, Hay House

French, G. (2012) The HighScope Approach to Early Learning, in M. Mahuna and M. Taylor (eds), *Early Childhood Education and Care: An Introduction for Students in Ireland*, Dublin, Gill and McMillan

Gaggi, O., Galiazzo, G., Palazzi, C., Facoetti, A. and Franceschini, S. (2012) A Serious Game for Predicting the Risk of Developmental Dyslexia in Pre-readers Children, paper presented at the 21st International Conference on Computer Communications and Networks (ICCCN), Munich, available online at: http://www.math.unipd.it/

Grieshaber, S. and McArdle, F. (2010) *The Trouble with Play*, Maidenhead, Open University Press/ McGraw-Hill Education

Harris, J., Golinkoff, R. and Hirsh-Pasek, K. (2011) Lessons from the Crib for the Classroom: How Children Really Learn Vocabulary, in S. Neuman and D. Dickinson, *Handbook of Early Literacy Research Vol. 3*, New York, The Guilford Press

Isaacs, B. (2015) *Bringing the Montessori Approach to your Early Years Practice* (3rd edn), Abingdon, David Fulton/Routledge

Jones, E. and Reynolds, G. (2015) *The Play's the Thing: Teachers' Roles in Children's Play*, 2nd edition, New York, Teachers College Press

MacKay, N. (2012), *Removing Dyslexia as a Barrier to Achievement* (3rd edn), Wakefield, SEN Marketing (www.senbooks.co.uk)

McNicholas, J. and McEntee, J. (1991, 2004) *Games to Improve Reading Levels*, NASEN/Routledge

Malaguzzi, L. (1994) Your Image of the Child: Where Teaching Begins (trans. B. Rankin, L. Morrow and L. Gandini), *Exchange*, 3, 1–5

Marshall, B. (2013) HighScope Today, Pedagogy for Learning and Development, in J. Georgeson, and J. Payler (eds), *International Perspectives on Early Childhood Education and Care*, Maidenhead, Open University Press/McGraw-Hill Education

Marshall, S. (1963) *An Experiment in Education*, Cambridge, Cambridge University Press, available online at: http://www.arvindguptatoys.com/

Mourgues, C., Preiss, D. and Grigorenko, E. (2014) Reading Skills, Creativity, and Insight: Exploring the Connections, *Spanish Journal of Psychology*, 17, 58, 1–10

Reid, G. (2005) Dyslexia, in A. Lewis and B. Norwich (eds), *Special Teaching for Special Children?*, Maidenhead, Open University Press

Ritchie, S. Luciano, M., Hansell, N., Wright, M. and Bates, T. (2013) The Relationship of Reading Ability to Creativity: Positive, not Negative Associations, *Learning and Individual Differences*, 26, 171–6

Robson, S. and Rowe, V. (2012) Observing Young Children's Creative Thinking: Engagement, Involvement and Persistence, *International Journal of Early Years Education*, 20, 4, 349–64

Saifer, S. (2010) Higher Order Play and Its Role in Development and Education, *Psychological Science and Education*, 3, 38–50

Steiner Waldorf Education (2011) *Guide to the Early Years Foundation Stage in Steiner Waldorf Early Childhood Settings*, Forest Row, Association of Steiner Waldforf Schools in the UK and Ireland

Woods, P., Ashley, M. and Woods, G. (2005) *Steiner Schools in England* (Research Report RR 645), Nottingham, DfES

Chapter 11

Dyslexia-aware practice for early childhood

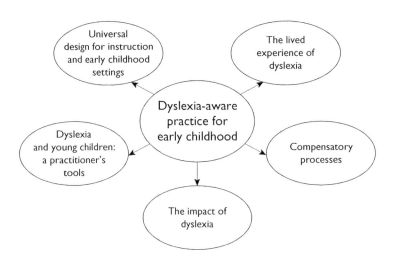

Good practice points

For good practice we need to:

1. develop good practice for learners with actual or potential dyslexia, as for all our learners, through evaluating and enhancing our own practice;
2. provide time and strategies for letters, numbers and processes that cause confusion for dyslexic learners;
3. record and evaluate our efforts to help children with potential or actual dyslexia in planning our next step;
4. plan ahead for dyslexic, or potentially dyslexic, learners who may come our way unexpectedly – what will we do?;
5. remember that dyslexia is lifelong; parents, caregivers and colleagues may also experience dyslexia and benefit from dyslexia-awareness.

The lived experience of dyslexia

Approaching the topic of dyslexia theory we might find ourselves confronted with two sets of ideas about where learning takes place. People who believe that the most important aspects of learning take place in brains (neuroscience) or minds (cognition) may talk about brain areas, links, activation, attention, memory, disorder and deficit. People who believe that the most important aspects of learning take place in social contexts may talk about communication, interaction, changing perceptions and the importance of environment or culture. These competing positions do not lend themselves easily to compromise.

There is a need to focus upon the daily, lived experience of dyslexia. Responsive teachers take account of social and cultural contexts, learning styles, and individual factors in their pedagogical efforts. In helping children to learn, they also seek to improve their own practice, and in the process they gain a repertoire of strategies. A responsive, dyslexia-aware practitioner is able to develop a plan to help a child who is struggling with literacy. Dyslexia-aware practitioners and caregivers can, by intensifying and modifying pedagogical activities consistently, have a beneficial impact upon actual or potential dyslexia.

Support for a child's emotional situation is crucially important. When children become aware of dyslexia, it is natural for them to want to be not-dyslexic and, for some, it is very difficult to put in the repetitious practice that is required to overcome dyslexia. Techniques, materials and resources that lift a child's spirits and engage their interest, promoting extra practice of literacy skills, are all valuable. Nevertheless, there is no 'quick fix' and the patient, systematic review of small pieces of literacy information may be frustrating and dispiriting for child and adult alike. Helping a child to maintain their equilibrium at times like this is an important task for adults. When a child requires input in the form of a structured, systematic dyslexia programme, this is likely to take place over a long period of time and a child needs to be resilient in order to cope with it.

Compensatory processes

Many people who experience dyslexia learn to manage it through the development of compensatory processes. As so often in discussions of dyslexia, there are internal and external aspects to this term. While some compensatory processes represent solutions to difficulties found by dyslexic people themselves, or, alternatively, strategies recommended during professional intervention, others are related to responsiveness and cognitive attention. Twentieth-century research into the neuroscience of dyslexia identified not only areas associated with reading and reading difficulty, but also other features of relevance. It gave support to the concept of 'plasticity' in human brains, a process indicating that when a neural area is hampered by injury or other reduced activation, different areas are sometimes able to compensate.

Possible neural differences among young dyslexic learners continue to be explored. For example, Raschle *et al.* (2012) found that differences in brain structure were present in young children at risk of dyslexia before they learned to read text. They found that areas associated with compensatory mechanisms for reading became evident later, as reading difficulties developed. Evans *et al.* (2014) found that there were consistent differences in the way dyslexic learners processed addition and subtraction tasks, even when particular mathematical difficulty or disability was not identified by testing. Bacon and Handley (2014) found that dyslexic learners placed greater reliance on remembering visual images. They relied on these rather than the verbal strategies of non-dyslexic learners. When learners who experienced dyslexia were able to use visual strategies, there was no difference in their actual reasoning ability, but visualisations were their main, compensatory strategies for reasoning.

Personal accounts are sometimes surprising in their descriptions of the compensatory strategies that dyslexic people may adopt in order to cope with literacy demands in daily life. It is possible to hear of individuals who approach a word from its far end, or who turn text upside-down, or who make links between letters or numerals and other items in order to help them to remember. These connections might seem complicated to practitioners who do not use compensatory strategies themselves, but they demonstrate the level of effort that a dyslexic learner may need to make in order to establish, in memory, even a small packet of information involving letters, words or numbers.

Compensatory strategies can include the range of facilitating activities that are available through the use of personal communication technology such as smart phones, and these are often discovered and shared by learners themselves. The term can also be used to describe the alternative processes that practitioners offer in order to help a learner to gain necessary literacy and numeracy skills. These include established techniques such as mnemonics, highlighting, reading aloud, Mind Mapping® and concept mapping. Dyslexia-aware practitioners can do more by paying particular attention to letters and numbers that can be confused easily, making sure that children's knowledge is secure.

It is uncertain whether neurological differences are causes, consequences or functions of dyslexia, and the extent to which arithmetical difficulty is related to dyslexia is still subject to research. However, the knowledge that there can be alternative ways of building neural connections for literacy and numeracy can encourage practitioners. Use of dyslexia-aware principles and methods, together with recognition of the importance of confidence in this area, will assist their practice.

The impact of dyslexia

Practitioners tend to be concerned with the impact of dyslexia upon a student's scholastic work, whereas for a student its impact is felt throughout daily life. We need constantly to interrogate our own practice, thinking about what it might mean for the lived experience of dyslexic learners. The impact that dyslexia has on a learner's confidence is more widely recognised today, as is the amount that can be achieved when students are encouraged, their confidence supported, and their literacy skills increased. Confidence comes from success, so what is needed is the opportunity to be successful. Dyslexic learners are engaged in a constant battle with a lack of success in literacy, an area that governs most of their educational experience, consequently confidence is continually undermined. As younger generations of students grow up in a climate where dyslexia is understood, and adjustments are made, it is to be hoped that schooling may become a more positive experience for them.

The impact of dyslexia is not only emotional; there is an economic impact. There is awareness of a relationship between poverty and dyslexia, but economic statistics reveal a starker picture. Serafino and Tonkin (2014) examine the impact of education on poverty as it is transmitted across generations; this is the concept of 'economic mobility'. Having a father whose education level is low is seven-and-a-half times more likely to have a negative impact upon a child's own educational outcomes, and consequently their financial wellbeing when they reach adulthood, than having a father with a moderate or high level of education. Similarly, a mother's low level of education makes this three times as likely (the authors note that previously mother's education had been thought of as more important). This is a statistical conclusion, not a case of blaming parents, and there are other factors involved. However, the authors conclude that, across the UK and Europe, parents', especially father's, low education level is the factor most likely to account for low education and poverty in the next generation.

In this context, the descriptors for the lowest level of education are 'cannot read and write', together with 'low attainment' (UNESCO international standard classification of education levels 0–2). There are many reasons why someone may not be able to read or write – lack of tuition, illness and difficult life events may all compromise literacy. Furthermore, being dyslexic does not necessarily mean that a person cannot read and write. Nevertheless, we cannot escape the conclusion that reduced literacy and low attainment in some cases will be the result of dyslexia. In these statistics we can see a pattern of educational attainment and poverty that makes it clear how important it is to help children to overcome dyslexia.

Dyslexia and young children: a practitioner's tools

In recent years, early years provision has come to be seen as a foundation for lifelong learning. Most particularly, early years provision operates against young children falling into a trap of poverty and inequality that is related to educational disadvantage. It has a social role; better education, starting with very young children, is important for the development of skills, opportunities and attitudes that support economic growth and employment. Within this social climate, the focus upon literacy has moved towards early identification and intervention, placing greater levels of responsibility upon adults who guide young learners.

Although there may be indicators and precursors, dyslexia is hard to verify until actual reading failure has taken place. A creative, responsive approach is required of practitioners when approaching matters of dyslexia in early childhood. There are a number of essential tools that practitioners can use across the range of early learning settings:

- *Communication*: Interaction and feedback with parents and caregivers is a practitioner's first tool. The help and understanding that is needed by a child with potential or actual dyslexia is not limited to schooling; it benefits from being a joint enterprise.
- *Observation*: Skilled observation is practitioners' second tool, seeing how a child learns, their skills and the setbacks they experience, the way they tackle a learning task, the things that are avoided and their development over time.
- *Empathic understanding*: Underpinning these, there needs to be a third tool – empathic understanding of what it feels like not to be able to do something, to be scared, or to hate the task. Practitioners can recall from their own childhood the learning areas that seemed insurmountably difficult for them and that made them feel miserable. In asking

how these tasks could have been made better for them, practitioners can use that knowledge to inform their practice.

- *Intervention*: Willingness to do something to help is practitioners' fourth tool, not just for a single occasion, but for a stated period of time. A professional approach would be to try an intervention for a month or half a term, monitoring and recording the outcomes and then evaluating it.
- *Strategies*: A repertoire of dyslexia-focused strategies is practitioners' fifth tool. The strategies for helping dyslexic children are well known – they include small, systematic steps, structured interventions, strategies that facilitate letter, sound, syllable, morpheme and word knowledge, multisensory approaches, rehearsal and revision of points learnt and the practice of teaching and learning that does not rely only on pencil and paper tasks. Strategies may include the use of specialised, systematic programmes.
- *Learning environment*: A good learning environment is practitioners' sixth tool. This includes: creating maximum clarity of letters and figures when used; showing minimum amounts of text at a time; moderating the amount of displays on a wall and the amount of wordage in them; reducing noise so that children can concentrate; and providing a quiet, stress-free corner for children who need that option.

If practitioners do all these things consistently, and a child's educational experience is stable and their attendance is good, then, if a child still struggles to gain literacy skills, the likelihood is increased that they experience potential or actual dyslexia. Much can be done by a sympathetic practitioner in a regular classroom. However, sometimes a practitioner's creativity and responsiveness are not enough on their own; all sources agree that for some dyslexic learners more is needed, and this generally refers to the need for a structured, systematic input. A small selection of text-based resources that can support both home and school work, used by practitioners and caregivers working together, is shown at Appendix 6.

Universal design for learning and early childhood settings

The universal design (UD) movement originated in the work of Ron Mace, combining architectural and access principles in championing available adjustments and accommodations for disabled people. Subsequently, this led to UD principles being applied to functions associated with non-disabled and neurotypical people and communities. Noting the level of interest in the UD concept among educators, McGuire *et al.* state: 'At a fundamental level, Universal Design has captured and illustrated an elusive element of inclusion: the anticipation and acknowledgement of human diversity as the norm' (McGuire *et al.*, 2006: 168). However, the authors also accept that there are some individuals who will need further adjustments and accommodations.

Educationally, the concept became known as universal design for instruction (UDI). The approach bears a kinship with dyslexia-friendly principles (Pavey, 2015), expressing similar approaches in a more formal way that applies to all disabilities and difficulties. The nine principles of UDI, applied to early childhood settings, are:

1. *equitable use*: practices are useful and accessible to all children;
2. *flexibility in use*: practitioners use the same means for all children – there is not a separate set of teaching and learning practices for a predetermined group;

3. *simple and intuitive*: input is not complicated unnecessarily, it is straightforward;
4. *perceptible information*: teaching and learning input is communicated effectively, whatever might be the difficulties or disabilities experienced by learners;
5. *tolerance for error*: practitioners accept that learners may have different foundational skills and a different pace of learning, and act accordingly – there is no 'blaming' culture;
6. *low physical effort*: learning is not arduous, physically;
7. *size and space for approach and use*: teaching and learning is arranged to take account of children's size, posture, mobility, reach and any communication needs;
8. *a community of learners*: communication is promoted, between children together and between children and practitioners;
9. *instructional climate*: this is 'welcoming and inclusive', with high expectations for children (adapted from Pavey, 2015, citing Scott *et al.*, 2003).

A setting where these principles are followed creates an optimum learning environment for all children. However, neither the inclusive principle of UDI nor that of the dyslexia-friendly initiative preclude the view that some learners will need additional specialist input.

Dyslexia-aware principles: summary

The preceding chapters show that, while it is difficult to identify potential or actual dyslexia in young children when they are only at a very early point in literacy, there are some features and characteristics that can alert us to the risk of dyslexia. The relationship of literacy with language is now more fully explored, and the links between dyslexia and early language shows us the importance of promoting language development. Having a parent who experiences dyslexia increases the chance of a child's dyslexia, but this chance is only around 50 per cent. From earliest stages we can be vigilant for the characteristics of learning differences that might indicate dyslexia among any of our learners, and respond to them with positive attitudes, understanding, empathy and a range of suitable techniques.

An example would be at the point where children start to be able to write independently. When children make the move from copying what an adult has written to being able to put a few words into a sentence for themselves, there is a point where an adult might think that transition is taking too long – months rather than weeks. A child might not be able to say back what an adult has written, failing to identify not just occasional words, but any of the words, every time, over a long duration. A practitioner might realise that, in spite of praise and encouragement, a child cannot recall even a single, small, meaningful word like 'I' that they have been copying for some time, in order to write it for themselves. These are all signs a practitioner should notice.

Whatever the future holds in terms of dyslexia theorisation or neurological research, it is possible to say that the way to work with dyslexic learners is now well known. It involves intensifying literacy learning and making input clear, vivid and multisensory, with a sense of the end result. It needs a sharpened perception of when logical, step-wise sequences, which are straightforward for educators, are too difficult for dyslexic learners. To aid children who are, or might be dyslexic to learn to read, write and spell requires knowledge of specific strategies, patient rehearsal and reiteration, and a continual process of reviewing our knowledge about dyslexia.

As a basic principle, we would want teaching and learning to take place within positive learning environments, where practitioners and learners can work together in good spirits. Confidence and resilience are important in helping children to overcome dyslexia, but gaining literacy skills also takes considerably more real effort for children who experience this. It can help if we put ourselves in the position of someone who is dyslexic and amend our practice accordingly. We need to listen to what children say about their own learning and to help them to sustain their efforts in the face of literacy difficulty.

Dyslexia-aware practice: evaluating our practice – a fidelity tool

The principles of UDI and principles of good practice for young children who experience potential or actual dyslexia in early years settings are combined in a fidelity tool for practitioners (Appendix 7). From the text of this book it draws three 'good practice' descriptors for each principle which we can match to our own practice, or we can substitute others if we prefer. The fidelity tool is for personal use, as a memory aid. Yearly review of the items, perhaps in discussion with a friend or colleague, helps us to remain aware of dyslexia-aware principles and think about what they mean for our practice.

Information and communication technology: augmentative and alternative communication

Assistive technology, providing augmentative and alternative communication (AAC) in the form of hardware and software, has been available for some time. Originally designed or adapted specially to help people who experience difficulties and disabilities, the development of modern communication platforms has seen many of these facilities move into mainstream use; adaptations previously used by dyslexic learners are becoming widespread. Although many of these facilities can be purchased as commercial products, there are free software programs available. Some adaptations are already installed in modern personal computers, located in the Access menu.

- *Speech recognition*: It has been difficult to provide speech recognition for children's voices because it has been hard for them to speak in the manner required; also, their voices change as they grow. However, this obstacle is being overcome and speech recognition is being used to create assessment programs, as well as reading and mathematics 'assistants'.
- *Text-to-speech*: Voices are increasingly lifelike and convincing. Children's voices are starting to be used, together with a range of languages and intonations, making the speech more accessible and interesting. Although specific software programs can be obtained, many web pages now have a facility for reading the screen, so that no separate software is required. A useful application is found in story-making programs such as Super Duper Story Maker (http://www.superduperinc.com/) or Pictello (www.assistiveware.com/).
- *Speech capability*: This has become important for smartphones and other devices. Speech input and output are now well established so that there can be verbal interaction with

'personal assistant' programs within mobile platforms; these include Siri (Apple operating platform), Cortana and Google Now (Microsoft). Speech capability is being used for toys; children can interact with their toys and have them respond to speech and touch.

- *Intelligent tutoring systems (ITS)*: An outcome of the technological advances in AAC is the development of intelligent tutoring systems whereby learners interact with the teaching and learning program; the program adjusts its responses following a child's verbal input. Furthermore, such programs can alter their response according to a participant's emotional state; for learners this can produce a positive approach and good outcomes (Ma *et al.*, 2014; Malekzadeh *et al.*, 2014). At the time of writing, ITS programs are experimental, but are of considerable interest to a number of major academic research centres. For example, iTalk2Learn is a European research project being carried out by a consortium of universities, with the aim of using ITS and 'robust learning' to develop mathematics teaching for five- to 11-year-old children. Project LISTEN, at Carnegie Mellon University, is aimed at improving literacy learning through an automated, talking tutor for reading.
- *Talking word processors*: There are a number of programs available that use text-to-speech for words written; some are free online. Clicker (www.cricksoft.com) is a commercially available program which has a longstanding reputation as a talking word processor for children's use, especially within the primary age range; it has been consistently recommended for learners who experience potential or actual dyslexia. Clicker 6 includes word prediction. It is available in a range of languages, including UK English and American English.

Developments in ICT such as these provide a range of support for young learners who experience potential or actual dyslexia. In new applications for AAC there is potential for speech and language development that can assist young learners. In addition, interactive reading programs offer opportunities for skills practice which are likely to engage and benefit dyslexic learners. Future developments offer the prospect of the teaching and learning of literacy acquiring a different character. This may be technological in nature, but it will be founded upon on a steady accumulation of research, practitioner expertise and pedagogic innovation derived from the study of dyslexia.

Learning games: incremental ladder games for supporting alphabetical knowledge

1. In a basic version, children work in pairs or small groups. They are given a paper or card drawn up like a ladder, with a sound/letter at the bottom and three rungs. They try to find short words that start with the same sound/letter, placing one on each rung. Sounds/letters chosen to start the ladder can correspond to those in a phonics sequence, or to commonly used sounds/letters, or to vowels, or to consonants, or to alphabetical knowledge, as preferred.

see
sun
sit
s

A fun element can be provided by distributing some words around the classroom at eye level, one for each ladder used, and allowing children to move round to them with their ladders, hunting for words if they cannot think of any themselves.

2. If children finish one ladder quickly, they can be given another.
3. Children who are starting to compile word lists, or use early dictionaries, can make a ladder of words that increase one letter at a time, so the first word has two letters, the second word has three and the third word has four letters.

stop
sun
so
s

4. Children who are learning alphabetical ordering can look for words that start with the same letter, but that have a second letter in alphabetical order.

swap
stop
see
s

5. Any of the above can be extended by providing ladders with more rungs.
6. Children can be challenged to make a sentence or a story from the ladder's words.

Adapted from McNicholas and McEntee (1991, 2004), no. 67: Ladder Game – Use of Dictionaries (p. 49) and no. 68: Ladder Race Game – Alphabetical Order (p. 50).

How can dyslexia be supported in these games?

- A dyslexia-aware practitioner avoids setting up a competitive aspect where children with potential dyslexia are disadvantaged or embarrassed by not being able to produce as much as others. A practitioner can avoid this by stating that the aim of the game is for every pair or group to complete a ladder and then to display them.
- If children wish to challenge themselves by completing more, or harder, or longer ladders, they can do so, and their achievements can be celebrated without a potentially dyslexic child feeling criticised.
- Individual children can go on complete ladders of their own if they wish. This would provide differentiation for a child who might be gifted in literacy, but it should not become a competition, otherwise a potentially dyslexic child would generally be likely to lose. This would undermine confidence at an early stage.
- A dyslexia-aware teacher never asks who could not manage the work. He or she makes sure that every child is able to manage the basic task.
- A practitioner can steer this game by providing ladders that start with letter/sounds and words that have already been practised and rehearsed.

- A practitioner can assist children who are struggling by making suggestions; the aim is to end up with three recognised words, not to identify children who cannot think of any. A dyslexia-aware practitioner will already know who might have trouble with this activity.
- To increase their interest value, completed ladders can be swapped around for other children to see and read.
- If children are asked to make a sentence or story from the ladder's words, this can be done verbally, giving a potentially dyslexic child a chance to demonstrate their imagination while the ladder's words supply visual and aural reinforcement.

Attitude, understanding, technique, empathy: how can I improve my practice?

This question derives from 'living theory', which McNiff and Whitehead (2010) present as the basis for 'action research'. In this approach, practitioners reflect upon and seek to develop their own practice. Improving our own dyslexia-aware practice includes:

- *attitude*: being willing to interrogate and audit our own practice regularly;
- *understanding*: knowing that dyslexia is found across the entire ability range; if a child is struggling in other learning, it does not mean that there is no dyslexia;
- *technique*: using the tools of communication, observation, intensification, monitoring, evaluation and strategic intervention without waiting for reading failure;
- *empathy*: appreciating that being gifted and talented, and dyslexic, can give rise to frustration and anxiety, and that keeping up with one's peers does not mean that there is no dyslexia.

Recommended reading

1. Wall, K. (2006) *Special Needs and Early Years* (2nd edn), London, SAGE
2. Hatcher, P., Duff, F. and Hulme, C. (2014) *Sound Linkage: An Integrated Programme for Overcoming Reading Difficulties*, Chichester, John Wiley and Sons
3. Reid, G. (2009) *Dyslexia, A Practitioner's Handbook* (4th edn), Chichester, John Wiley and Sons (and subsequent editions)

Useful websites

1. http://www.cricksoft.com/
   Crick Software is the manufacturer of Clicker 6. Clicker has a number of apps available for home or school use with iPad. Crick Software makes free software available via http://www.learninggrids.com/uk/ (registration required).
2. http://www.commonsensemedia.org/
   This is the website of a non-profit organisation in the USA that makes advice and information about technology available to parents, caregivers and educators.
3. http://www.inspiration.com/
   Inspiration is the name of the company that produces Kidspiration 3, a software program for graphic representations. This employs visual learning to help children to accomplish thinking and learning in literacy in ways that are not text-heavy. The program links directly with classroom whiteboards if required and is available in different ICT formats. A free trial is available on the website.

MY DYSLEXIA EXPERIENCE: NAVIGATING SCHOOL WITH A DYSLEXIC
CHILD (CONT.)

My son will say that one of the most important decisions he made as a dyslexic student was to embrace the diagnosis. I remember when he first heard the name. He actually loved the label. He felt it contained the condition. He revelled in the realization that dyslexia didn't make him stupid. It was a specific learning glitch, but it didn't impact his entire brain. (Redford, 2014)

References

Bacon, A. and Handley, S. (2014) Reasoning and Dyslexia: Is Visual Memory a Compensatory Resource?, *Dyslexia*, 20, 4, 330–45

Evans, T., Flowers, D., Napoliello, E., Olulade, O. and Eden, G. (2014) The Functional Anatomy of Single-digit Arithmetic in Children with Developmental Dyslexia, *Neuroimage*, 101, 644–52

Hatcher, P., Duff, F. and Hulme, C. (2014) *Sound Linkage: An Integrated Programme for Overcoming Reading Difficulties*, Chichester, John Wiley and Sons

Ma, W., Adesope, O., Nesbit, J. and Liu, Q. (2014) Intelligent Tutoring Systems and Learning Outcomes: A Meta-Analysis, *Journal of Educational Psychology*, 106, 4, 901–18

McGuire, J., Scott, S. and Shaw, S. (2006) Universal Design and its Applications in Educational Environments, *Remedial and Special Education*, 27, 3, 166–75

McNiff, J. and Whitehead, J. (2010) *You and Your Action Research Project*, Abingdon, Routledge

McNicholas, J. and McEntee, J. (1991, 2004) *Games to Improve Reading Levels*, NASEN/Routledge

Malekzadeh, M., Salim, S. and Mustafa, M. (2014) Towards Integrating Emotion Management Strategies in Intelligent Tutoring System Used by Children, in P. Cipresso, A. Matik and G. Lopez (eds), *Pervasive Computing Paradigms for Mental Health, Fourth International Symposium, MindCare 2014*, Tokyo, Springer International

Pavey, B. (2015) The UK's Dyslexia-friendly Initiative and the USA's Universal Design Movement: Exploring a Possible Kinship, *Asia Pacific Journal of Developmental Differences*, 2, 1, 39–54

Raschle, N., Zik, J. and Gaab, N. (2012) Functional Characteristics of Developmental Dyslexia in Left-hemispheric Posterior Brain Regions Predate Reading Onset, *Proceedings of the National Academy of Sciences (PNAS)*, 109, 6, 2156–61

Redford, K. (2014) *Navigating School with a Dyslexic Child*, New Haven, CT, Yale Center for Dyslexia and Creativity, available online at: http://dyslexia.yale.edu/PAR_NavigatingSchool.html

Reid, G. (2009) *Dyslexia: A Practitioner's Handbook* (4th edn), Chichester, John Wiley and Sons

Scott, S., McGuire, J. and Shaw, S. (2003) Universal Design for Instruction: A New Paradigm for Adult Instruction in Postsecondary Education, *Remedial and Special Education*, 24, 6, 369–79

Serafino, P. and Tonkin, R. (2014) *Intergenerational Transmission of Disadvantage in the UK and EU*, London, Office for National Statistics

Wall, K. (2006) *Special Needs and Early Years* (2nd edn), London, SAGE

A selection of published assessment tools relevant for literacy/dyslexia

This small selection of published tests for younger children is for use by teachers with training in the administration and scoring of assessment instruments. Examples are offered for different facets of literacy; other tests are available. A list of assessment tools approved for assessing characteristics related to dyslexia, showing age ranges for the tests, can be found at the website for the SpLD Assessment Standards Committee (SASC), http://www.sasc.org.uk/, under the heading Revised Guidelines.

Cognition

Lucid Research Ltd. (1996) *Cognitive Profiling System (CoPS)*, Beverley, Lucid Research Ltd.

> For children aged four to eight years, this computerised screener seeks to identify dyslexic tendencies before and during reading acquisition.

Glutting, J., Adams, W. and Sheslow, D. (2000) *Wide Range Intelligence Test (WRIT)*, Wilmington, DE, Wide Range, Inc.

> A test for individuals aged four to 85 years.

Memory and learning

Sheslow, D. and Adams, W. (2003) *Wide Range Assessment of Memory and Learning: Revised (WRAML 2)*, Wilmington, DE, Wide Range, Inc.

> A test for individuals aged five to 90 years.

Reynolds, C. and Bigler, E. (2001) *Test of Memory and Learning* (2nd edn) (*TOMAL 2*), Belford, Ann Arbor

> A test for individuals aged five years to 59 years 11 months.

Vocabulary

Dunn, L., Dunn. D., Styles, B. and Sewell, J. (2009) *British Picture Vocabulary Scale, 3rd edition (BPVS 3)*, London, GL Assessment

> For ages three to 16 years, this assessment of receptive vocabulary requires no reading or speaking from a child.

Phonological difficulties

Gibbs, S. and Bodman, S. (2014) *Phonological Assessment Battery 2nd Edition Primary (PhAB 2 Primary)*, Swindon, GL Assessment

> For ages five to11 years. This revised version of PhAB assesses phonological and lexical-semantic processes.

Wagner, R., Torgesen, J., Rashotte, C. and Pearson, N. (2013) *Comprehensive Test of Phonological Processing, 2nd edition (CCTOP 2)*, Austin, PRO-ED Inc.

> This test assesses phonological abilities and processing skills. The revised version lowers the age range for the test to four to six years. The ceiling for the test is 24 years 11 months.

Reading

Forum for Research into Language and Literacy (2012) *Diagnostic Test of Word Reading Processes (DTWRP)*, London, GL Assessment

> For children aged six to 12 years, this assesses reading ability using phonological and lexical-semantic processes.

Hulme, C., Stothard, S., Clarke, P., Bowyer-Crane, C., Harrington, A., Truelove, E. and Snowling, M. (2009) *York Assessment of Reading Comprehension (YARC): Early Reading*, London, GL Assessment

> For ages four to seven years, this assesses phonological skills, alphabetic knowledge and word reading. Test scoring is available through the publisher's website (http://www.gl-assessment.co.uk/)

Dyslexia

Turner, M. and Smith, P. (2003) *Dyslexia Screener*, London, GL Assessment

> Dyslexia Screener digital is also available. For ages five to 16+ years, Dyslexia Screener identifies dyslexic tendencies and recommends strategies.

Fawcett, A. and Nicolson, R. (2004) *Dyslexia Early Screening Test (2nd edition) (DEST 2)*, Oxford, Pearson Education

> This assessment tool was developed from the cerebellar theory of dyslexia. It is suitable for children aged four years six months to six years five months.

Movement tracking, timed: room plan with activity duration (adapted from Wall, 2006: 119)

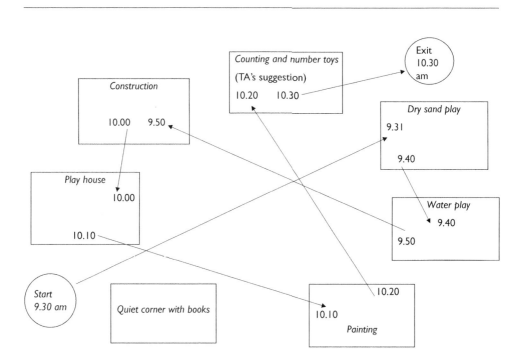

Timed observation record

Name of child observed .... Age ......Date of observation............

Focus/objective of observation...

Context in which observation took place...

Duration of observation and time intervals..

Observer(s)...

Time of observation	What is observed child doing?	What is teacher doing?	What is teaching assistant doing?	What are the other children doing?

Additional notes (continue over)...............

Personal approval/disapproval monitoring chart

| Context/setting details: |
| Date: |

Days	Instances of approval (verbal, gesture, smile)	Total	Instances of disapproval (criticism, reprimand)	Total
1				
2				
3				
4				
5				
6				
7				
8				
9				
10				
Grand totals				

Ratio of approval : disapproval

Were any behaviour changes noted in yourself or anyone else?

Could anything else have caused the changes, other than approval/disapproval experiences?

A dyslexia-aware multiplication table

2 x table ☆☆

1 x 2 = 2
2 x 2 = 4

3 x 2 = 6
4 x 2 = 8

5 x 2 = 10
6 x 2 = 12

7 x 2 = 14
8 x 2 = 16

9 x 2 = 18
10 x 2 = 20

11 x 2 = 22
12 x 2 = 24

1 x 2 = 2
2 x 2 = 4
3 x 2 = 6
4 x 2 = 8
5 x 2 = 10
6 x 2 = 12
7 x 2 = 14
8 x 2 = 16
9 x 2 = 18
10 x 2 = 20
11 x 2 = 22
12 x 2 = 24

Appendix 6

Some text-based resources

These titles represent only a small number out of a vast array of products designed to address literacy difficulties. Many of the materials consist of a number of volumes and workbooks, but only one relevant example for any series is given here.

Some frequently used, phonics-based reading/literacy programmes

For UK use:

Department for Education and Skills (DfES) (2007) *Letters and Sounds: Principles and Practice of High Quality Phonics*, Nottingham, DfES
A free resource, available online at: https://www.gov.uk/

Hatcher, P., Duff, F. and Hulme, C. (2014) *Sound Linkage: An Integrated Programme for Overcoming Reading Difficulties*, Chichester, John Wiley and Sons

Miskin, R. and Archbold, T. (2007) *Phonics Flashcards (Read Write Inc. Phonics)*, Oxford, Oxford University Press
Ruth Miskin's Read Writ Inc. materials are available through the website at: http://www.ruthmiskin.com

Wernham, S. and Lloyd, S. (2010) *Jolly Phonics Teacher's Book*, Chigwell, Jolly Learning
Materials are available through the website, in UK and USA formats, at: http://www.jollylearning.co.uk/

For USA use:

Blachman, B., Ball, E., Black, R. and Tangel, D. (2000) *Road to the Code: A Phonological Awareness Program for Young Children*, Baltimore, Brookes

Some current systematic phonics programmes for use with learners who experience dyslexia

For UK use:

Combley, M. (2000) *The Hickey Multisensory Language Course* (3rd edn), Chichester, Wiley-Blackwell

Hornsby, B., Frear, S. and Pool J. (2006) *Alpha to Omega Teacher's Handbook* (6th edn), Harlow, Heinemann/Dyslexia Action

Kelly, K. and Phillips, S. (2011) *Teaching Literacy to Learners with Dyslexia*, London, SAGE

For USA use:

Traub, N. and Bloom, F. (2000) *Recipe for Reading (Revised and Expanded)* (3rd edition), Cambridge, MA, Educators Publishing Service Company (EPS)

Clark-Edmands, S. (2005) *SPIRE Teacher's Guide Level 1* (2nd edn), Cambridge, MA, Educators Publishing Service Company (EPS)

Grammar and spelling

For UK use:

Department for Children, Schools and Families (DCSF) (2010) *Support for Spelling*, Nottingham, DCSF

Includes CD-ROM.

Wernham, S. and Lloyd, S. (2007) *The Grammar 1 Handbook* (2nd edn), Chigwell, Jolly Learning
Includes photocopiable resources.

For USA use:

Hall, N. (2005) *Explode the Code: Teachers Guide for Books A, B, C*, Cambridge, MA, Educators Publishing Service Company (EPS)

Shared use between home and school

Broomfield, H. (2004) *Overcoming Dyslexia Resource Book 1*, London, Whurr
Includes photocopiable resources.

Cowling, H. (2004) *The Hornet Literacy Primer*, Staningsley, Wasp

Franks, E., Nicholson, M. and Stone, C. (2007) *Beat Dyslexia: A Step-by-step Multi Sensory Literacy Programme, Book 1*, Nottingham, LDA

Appendix 7

Fidelity and self-evaluation tool for promoting dyslexia-aware practice for young children

		page one
Good practice points	Strategy	Do I do this now?
1. Equitable use: practices are useful and accessible to all children		
I hear reading myself, regularly		
I link new learning to previous learning		
I keep my classroom quiet for literacy and numeracy		
2. Flexibility in use: practitioners use the same means for all children		
I use dyslexia-aware principles in all my practice		
I provide a range of materials for mark-making		
I provide a range of materials for creative work		
3. Simple and intuitive: input is not complicated unnecessarily, it is straightforward		
I know 10 dyslexia-focused activities to help reading		
I know 10 dyslexia-focused activities to help writing		
I know 10 dyslexia-focused activities to help spelling		

	page two
4. Perceptible information: teaching and learning input is communicated effectively	
I differentiate learning tasks	
I make my voice as clear as possible without shouting	
I keep literacy and numeracy work clear, uncrowded and easy to read	
5. Tolerance for error: acceptance that learners may have different foundational skills and a different pace of learning	
I avoid blaming or criticising children with literacy difficulties	
I work to improve my praise to criticism/ reprimand ratio	
I correct errors by using explanations	
6. Low physical effort: learning is not arduous physically	
I offer children the chance to shine in other areas	
I provide opportunities for play	
I watch for signs of children's avoidance or difficulty in my setting	
7. Size and space for approach and use: teaching and learning takes account of children's size, posture, mobility, reach and communication needs	
I provide a range of print experiences for children, such as large and small books, large-print books, picture-only books and talking texts	
I provide a range of large- and small-scale multisensory equipment and toys	
Children are not denied enjoyable activities because of the standard of their written work	

8. A community of learners: communication is promoted, between children together and between children and practitioners	
I encourage active listening	
I encourage children to talk in sentences	
I avoid closing conversations down too soon	
9. Instructional climate: welcoming and inclusive, with high expectations for children	
I use playfulness and good humour, without teasing, to keep us all in good spirits	
I challenge children's thinking, asking them to plan, predict, discuss ideas and alternatives, evaluate, make judgements, and say why they have made them	
I involve parents and caregivers in efforts to support literacy, taking care to include parents whose first language is not English	

Top 3 Targets

1..

2..

3..

(Signed)... (date)...............................

Index

Printed in Great Britain
by Amazon